I0003967

How to Alleviate

Digital Transformation Debt

post- **COVID-19**

How to Alleviate

Digital Transformation Debt

post- C VID-19

Dr. Setrag Khoshafian

Columbus, Ohio

How to Alleviate Digital Transformation Debt post-COVID-19

Published by Gatekeeper Press
2167 Stringtown Rd, Suite 109
Columbus, OH 43123-2989
www.GatekeeperPress.com

Library of Congress Control Number: 2021935746

ISBN (hardcover): 9781662912030
ISBN (paperback): 9781662912047
eISBN: 9781662912054

Table of Contents

Preface

2020 - the year of the COVID-19 pandemic - changed everything.

Its ripple effects will be felt for many years to come.

At the same time, there have been incredible advances in digitization. We are amid a digital revolution with unprecedented innovations. The pandemic has accelerated the *requirements* for "Digital Transformation." Organizations need to adapt and transform to survive and hopefully thrive.

At the core of digitization, there is very much an underlying principle of "debt." It comes originally from what Is called "technical debt." Simply put, technical debt "reflects the implied cost of additional rework caused by choosing an easy solution now instead of using a better approach that would take longer." Difficult transformative choices need to be made *now*—especially post-COVID-19. If an organization ignores digital transformation for "easy solutions," the "debt" accumulates and can have disastrous consequences.

The pandemic has accelerated the accumulation of Digital Transformation Debt!

It has also provided an opportunity to thrive in the post-COVID-19 era.

What does Digital Transformation mean? What are the opportunities? What are the core digital technologies? What are the best practices? What are practical recommendations to alleviate the Digital Transformation Debt?

This book addresses Digital Transformation Debt holistically and makes recommendations on how to alleviate the debt. Here is the outline:

Chapter 1: The book starts with the need to transform the organizational Culture.

Chapter 2: To thrive in this milieu, organizations need to address optimizations for their processes or *value streams*.

Chapter 3: The value streams and all operations need to be Automated. There is a spectrum of automation for all categories of work.

Chapter 4: Software runs the world. A new category of programming is transforming organizations, primarily through the emergence of Citizen Developers.

Chapter 5: Organizations are becoming Data-centric. Extracting Data insights to improve the enterprise is becoming critical. Citizen Data Scientist are the agents for data transformation.

Chapter 6: Only the Innovators will survive. Methodologies such as Design Thinking and Minimum Viable Products best practices need to be weaved in the organization's DNA.

Chapter 7: Customer behaviors have changed radically. Significant shifts in Customer Experience and the powerful voice of the new generation of customers change all the priorities.

Chapter 8: The world is becoming increasingly connected through IoT. Connected devices have permeated homes, businesses, cities, and governments as well Manufacturing: IIoT.

Chapter 9: The world is also becoming *Decentralized.* Internet of Things is supplemented with the Internet of Value through Blockchain and Decentralized applications.

Chapter 10: Digital Organizations need to balance Innovation with Best Practices. The Competency Centers with empowered roles will play a key role in governance, enablement and methodologies alleviating DTD.

Author

Dr. Setrag Khoshafian has been a senior executive in the digital industry, where he has innovated, architected, and led the development of several digital transformation products, services, and solutions.

Dr. Khoshafian is a pioneer and recognized expert in Intelligent Databases and Intelligent Business Process Management.

His expertise spans Process Automation, IoT/IIoT, Blockchain, Low Code/No Code, AI, Design Thinking, and Competency Centers.

He is a frequent speaker at international conferences. His TEDx talk covers the importance of Culture over Technology.

Dr. Khoshafian is the author of more than 10 books - including the seminal *Service Oriented Enterprises* - and hundreds of business and academic articles in recognized journals.

Tweet: @setrag

LinkedIn: https://www.linkedin.com/in/setrag/

Chapter 1: Culture

The impact of the Covid-19 lockdown of businesses and government will be felt for many years to come. It is causing mega-cultural trends that are already changing us. We might not be feeling or appreciating the *shifts* that are happening. It is too close to home, and we are in the midst of it.

But it is happening, and it is very real.

Digitization has already been transforming all aspects of our lives, even pre-COVID-19. But the pandemic has certainly catalyzed these technological and cultural changes.

COVID-19 is catalyzing the rapid acceleration of Digital Transformation (DX) initiatives

According to the COVID-19 digital engagement report from Twilio [1]: *Decade-long digital transformation roadmaps of nearly every company got compressed into days and weeks in order to curb the spread of the Coronavirus. Businesses in every industry had to figure out how to reach their customers - whether those customers are shoppers, patients, students, businesses or even, employees - essentially overnight."*

This certainly underscores the importance of Digital Transformation Debt. COVID-19, then, has re-prioritized, stressed, and accelerated digital transformation change.

In 2018, I wrote a two-part article on Digital Transformation Debt (DTD) with the premise that if organizations do not address their "Debts"—the challenges we are facing from all fronts—they will pay a much heftier price: even an existential one. Recently, Cisco's former CEO, John Chambers, indicated that 50% of Fortune 500 companies would not exist in 10 years [2]. Even if we ignore DTD, companies were already on a downward spiral, and the pandemic is making these matters much worse. The need to "change" (here we go again) is not a luxury, and it cannot be ignored. The main principle of "debt" is ignoring this painful transformational change in favor of easy and often delayed solutions. Ignoring the trends and choosing the path of least resistance will only accumulate "the Debt." This applies to Technical Debt, but especially in the COVID-19 era, it refers to DTD.

In Part I [3] of the two-part article, I covered the following dimensions:

1. Organizational Culture
2. Value Stream Digitization
3. Intelligent Automation
4. Citizen Developers
5. Citizen Data Scientists

Part II [4] covered:

6. Design Thinking
7. Customer Experience Optimization
8. The Connected World
9. The Decentralized World
10. Digital Transformation Centers of Excellence (COE)

All ten dimensions are relevant, but how has COVID-19 impacted these dimensions? And how about the importance and priority of Digital Transformation Debt (DTD)?

> *Addressing Digital Transformation Debt has become much more critical in the post-COVID-19 era.*

In 2020, I published a ten-part series on Cognitive World [5], expanding on the post-COVID-19 impact for each of the dimensions: starting with Culture and culminating with Digital Transformation Competence Centers. This book is based on these ten articles.

The pandemic has served as a rude awakening. Organizations of all sizes simply cannot take "business as usual" for granted. Addressing core cultural challenges has become critical – it is a matter of survival.

Given the critical importance of DTD, this is the first of the series that will focus on the ten dimensions.

Post-COVID-19 Culture

The importance of Culture was accentuated in the post-COVID-19 era. Indeed, true transformation starts with Culture. One of the most archaic organizational structures that have survived decades if not centuries is the ubiquitous vertical "Org Chart." The conventional hierarchical "Org Chart" does not inspire agility, change, or empowerment in the pre-COVID-age.

Post-COVID-19, this has been challenged and stressed to the limit. It is no longer a working model, especially with the newer, technologically savvy, independent-minded, and entrepreneurial younger generations.

> *The impact on Organization Culture is one of the most fascinating realities of the post-COVID-19 digital era.*

Digital Technologies are just enablers of cultural trends that are transforming all demographics at an accelerated rate.

> *Culture is always more important and impactful than pure digital technologies, as impressive as the latter are.*

The potential cultural impacts on individuals as well as organizations are tremendous. To succeed and innovate with digitization, transformation best practices should challenge long-established cultural norms *and* hierarchical structures.

Hierarchies thrive on management layers exerting control, functioning through power-driven bureaucratic practices, and suffocating innovation, if not the organization's very life! The digital era fosters challenging the hierarchical and centralized control-driven organizations with alternative, more democratic robust models that empower the participants.

Connecting through Virtualization

Gone are the days of the online and offline worlds being separate. Today's new reality is marked by *virtuality*. Indeed, the shift toward a virtual presence and virtual interactions is a mega digital transformational trend that will impact enterprises of all sizes forever. Video conferencing tools such as Zoom, Cisco Webex, Microsoft Teams, GoToMeeting, and others have witnessed a surge in downloads and use. Virtual conferencing and the use of virtual conferencing tools is at least an order of magnitude far higher than in pre-COVID-19 times. For example, a recent survey has indicated that 72% of consumers [6] had their first-ever virtual care visit during the COVID-19 pandemic. Zoom has become a household name and one of the most popular video conferencing platforms to date, though all the others have witnessed significant growth as well. One of my favorite video conferencing tools that I use almost daily is Facebook's Portal – it even has several original games and stories weaved in. Though more for personal and family use, I have used it for professional meetings, and the results are pretty good. Such widespread use of video conferencing tools – both for business and personal matters – will have a long-lasting impact on organizations and individuals for decades to come.

Flattening the Organization

The emergence of virtual meetings with full virtual presence has engendered an *equalizing* and flattening

effect on most orga-
nizations. Suddenly,
all the organizational
hierarchy levels have
become accessible,
and physical restri-
ctions – such as the
number of people
who can physically be
hosted in a conference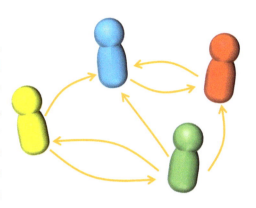
room or even the availability of conference rooms for
interactions – have been lifted. The speed of organizing
virtual meetings, their accessibility, and the ability to
record and then analyze them are other key advantages
that have a flattening and potentially empowering
impact on the organization – especially if management
encourages and endorses it. The top-down pyramid and
functional unit organization structures are antiquated
and passé in our new age of technological marvel. They
do not inspire innovation or digital transformation.
Employee empowerment has been elusive and hard to
achieve within a rigidly hierarchical organization. The
COVID-19 pandemic provides a wonderful opportunity
for organizations to re-assess their rigid structures and
flatten their organizations.

> *Flattening organizations with increased
> communication, collaboration, and
> empowerment is an irreversible trend.*

We are and will continue to face many labor challenges in the post-COVID-19 era. A digital and agile organization with enough empowerment can leverage its employees' innovative talents and improve their overall morale. The idea of challenging hierarchical structures, removing bosses (or replacing them with "mentors") has been teasing us for a while. The need to quickly change and adapt to become *digital* enterprises is compelling businesses and organizations to re-consider their rigid structures.

The Home Office Experience

The culture shift is markedly complex and multi-faceted. The cultural reset of "normal" work in a compelling survey [7] had some impressive results. It indicated that after the imposed lockdown, employees want greater flexibility in the percentage of time they spent at home vs. office – the breakdown is 51% office and 49% home – thus, almost half of society wishes to work from home. Other trends included a focus on results vs. hours of labor: the end of the 9-5 model, changes in leadership attitudes, and desire to be upskilled. In other words, the employment world will be quite different post-pandemic.

- Trust and Empowerment [8]: Working from home has fostered a milieu of trust and productivity. In some traditional hierarchical organizations, managers wanted to physically "observe" employees at work. Now, that is still possible (through monitoring technologies) for the home office. However, increasingly, managers realize that the focus on productivity vs. control of physical presence is a much better approach – capable of yielding far better results. Some managers and HR within many organizations are realizing they need to be more pro-active in trusting and empowering their employees vs. the micro-management that is so pervasive in traditional hierarchical organizations. The survey mentioned above indicated the individual autonomy of scheduling work increased from 7% to 22% - resulting in a much higher demand for flexibility. It hinges on trust and empowerment. This shift is a positive development in the cultural transformation. Its impact will undoubtedly be appreciated for decades to come.

- Stress [9]: Working from home alleviated some stress, particularly stemming from the long hours of commute for some. But it has also, inadvertently, created others. Lockdown and quarantine have blurred the boundary between home and work, which has sometimes created tension within homes. Managers and HR had to mentor employees on balancing personal life and work. We are starting to see best practices and a lot of experimentation of different approaches to alleviate these stressful situations for employees. Some strategies include frequent and on-point communication, clear and repeated articulation of available resources to mitigate stress, and pro-active guidance – especially for employees who find it challenging to work from home due to a plethora of personal reasons. Managers and C-level executives need to place empathy, trust, and wellbeing at the forefront of the post-COVID-19 Culture.

Recommendations

What should organizations do to alleviate the Cultural aspect of DTD – which is perhaps the most important one? The hierarchy needs to be turned upside-down, with the traditional higher-ups serving the organization's most Important assets: the employees. In essence, becoming *servant leaders.*

> *Enterprises need to lead by example in changing their Culture, pioneering this cultural shift toward a more egalitarian style of leadership.*

A servant leader's primary focus is to serve – not to manage or control. Servant leaders do not operate by imposing their opinions on others. Instead, their aim is to serve the needs and objectives of the employees. In this leadership dynamic, the pyramid is reversed. At the apex are those people or organizations one is trying to serve. The "leader" is at the base.

Here are the characteristics of the *flattened organization* with servant leadership [10]:

- *Focus on Serving and Empowering*: As noted above, servant leaders do not try to force their approaches. Instead, they attempt to serve the aspirations of the people they manage. The pyramid is reversed.

- *Sharing the Organization's Vision:* Servant leaders communicate and share their vision. The employees know what part they are playing in a big picture. That motivates them.

- *Teamwork:* Servant leaders believe in and promote teamwork in which each member contributes and collaborates for a common goal.

- *Building Communities:* Servant leaders attempt to build communities and prioritize relationship building. Servant leaders realize that if workers and partners like and enjoy each other, the productivity and quality of work will greatly improve.

- *Mentoring and Development:* Servant leaders are committed to mentoring their employees and focus on their professional development.

- *Encouragement Focused:* Servant leaders are positive leaders. They constantly appreciate and encourage their employees as well as other communities that they serve.

- *Balanced*: Servant leaders realize work is just a means to produce income; not an end. Servant leaders believe in and promote a balanced perspective on life and priorities.

- *Practical and Rational*: Servant leaders prefer to focus on exceptions and needs vs. legalism. They take a pragmatic approach when it comes to providing the right resources for their employees.

Now there are many existing and emerging digital technologies that help and accelerate each of these characteristics of servant leadership. However, the focus should be on the mind frame and cultural change within the organization - starting at the "top." Technology can help only as a support tool.

These should be the highest priorities in the post-COVID-19 era. The executive board, then, needs to make it the main strategic priority. Managers, C-levels, and vice presidents need to go through a process of rigorous education, training, certification, and evaluation in Servant Leadership. The Greenleaf Center for Servant Leadership [11] is an excellent place to start.

References

[1]   https://www.twilio.com/covid-19-digital-engagement-report

[2]   https://www.sdxcentral.com/articles/news/john-chambers-50-of-fortune-500-wont-exist-in-10-years/2020/06/

[3]   https://www.forbes.com/sites/cognitiveworld/2018/09/04/digital-transformation-debt-part-i/?sh=20f864ae2e8d

[4]   https://www.forbes.com/sites/cognitiveworld/2018/09/14/digital-transformation-debt-part-ii/?sh=3a2025fb112d

[5]   https://cognitiveworld.com/articles/category/Setrag+Khoshafian

[6]   https://www.biospace.com/article/releases/ge-healthcare-deploys-remote-patient-data-monitoring-technology-to-help-clinicians-support-most-critical-covid-19-patients-across-the-health-system/

[7]   https://www.adeccogroup.com/research-block/reset-normal/

[8]   https://www.fastcompany.com/90483201/5-ways-to-build-trust-when-your-teams-are-working-from-home-indefinitely

[9]   https://www.cultureamp.com/blog/how-covid-19-is-changing-the-employee-experience/

[10] https://www.amazon.com/Service-Oriented-Enterprises-Setrag-Khoshafian/dp/0849353602

[11] https://www.greenleaf.org/

Chapter 2: Operational Excellence

These are economically challenging times for all of us. Indeed, organizations face tremendous uphill battles in cutting costs and *becoming lean* – while still delivering high-quality products and services. In subsequent chapters, we shall also cover innovation and entrepreneurship, which are essential for survival.

Value Stream digitization and automation (discussed in the next Chapter) in the post-COVID-19 era has two salient dimensions:

(1) Operational Excellence, particularly for customer service and the associated intra-Enterprise processes.

(2) Inter-Enterprise Collaboration through Value-Stream-As-A-Service (defined below).

There are considerable challenges in addressing both. A joint study by McKinsey and Harvard Business School showed – not too surprisingly – that organizations that maintained an agile model before COVID-19 fared much better [1].

This Chapter will delve deeper into how enterprises can become "agile enterprises." Many enterprises have attempted but failed to transform themselves, especially achieving the appropriate velocity of innovation and change. They have accumulated Digital Transformation Debt – and it weighs on them. The focus in this chapter is on leaning the enterprise through operational excellence.

Operational Excellence: Real-Time Lean Six Sigma

The current economic downturn caused by COVID-19 has provided business process re-engineering [2] (yes, it is back) opportunities to organizations – giving them the space to rethink and change both their operational as well as customer and partner-centric end-to-end value streams. In other words, they are improving their processes – primarily due to factors such as downsizing, loss of revenue, and challenges in the supply chain: all as the result of the COVID-19 lockdown.

The problem of silos remains ever-pervasive, and it is safe to say that the COVID-19 lockdown itself exposed the silo vulnerabilities *big time*. Many organizations have faced, and are still facing, challenges that threaten their very existence. However, the shakeup caused by the pandemic can also be interpreted in a more optimistic sense: as a catalyst for innovation – especially in Operational Excellence. There are compelling pressures on organizations of different sizes to re-visit and optimize their operations. Now more than ever, there is a sense of urgency to find a common language between IT – Business – Operations and avoid waste.

> *Post-COVID-19 enterprises need to be continuously in motion through optimizing operations.*

Enterprises, by their very nature, are complex systems. The ecosystems of enterprises are becoming more complex. Even medium and small-sized enterprises have too many moving parts. Silos and the absence of meaningful coordination could thus cause serious inefficiencies.

Consider how service provisioning has changed over the past few years. Each of the following showed vulnerabilities—and opportunities—in the COVID-19 era:

- Mitigating and remediating risks during times of uncertainty.

- Complying with regulations and optimizing the audit processes.

- Resolving potential disputes by connecting the increasingly demanding customer to the rest of the enterprise nodes in real-time.

- Manufacturing end-to-end new products and services at an accelerated pace.

Organizations involve a collection of *Value Streams*. A Value Stream (aka Value Chain) is a business process that orchestrates activities (aka tasks) of people, applications, robots, etc. for specific business objectives. Here is robust

way to categorize the value streams in an organization: Support Value Streams (IT help desks, HR, Finance, Legal, etc.); Mission Critical Value Streams (Production, Marketing, Sales, Support, etc.); and Management Value Streams (Performance Management, Strategy Management, etc.). Digitization and Operational

Excellence pertains to all layers – but most notably to Mission Critical Value Streams.

iBPM for Digitizing and Automating Value Streams

Intelligent Business Process Management (iBPM) platforms have become powerful tools for the development of Low Code/No Code (more details in Chapter 4) process-centric intelligent applications. The value proposition of iBPM with technology and best practices for orchestrating People, Connected Things (aka IoT - Chapter 8), Enterprises Applications, and Trading Partners is critical in the post-COVID-19 era.

iBPM has evolved, often with confusing categories such as Digital Process Automation, Dynamic Case Management, High-Productivity Application Platform as a Service, Enterprise Low Code, Robotic Process Automation – to name a few. The new generation of iBPM incorporates – either natively or through partnerships – many

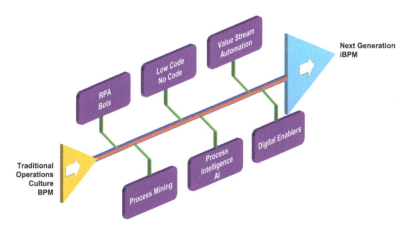

capabilities, as illustrated here. Digital Enables include Cloud, Social, Mobile, Internet of Things, and, most recently, Blockchain.

How about Value Stream digitization and automation?

The success and indeed the survival rate of enterprises will very much depend upon the robust digitization of their Value Streams (aka Value Chains – we will use the terms interchangeably). Borrowing a compelling perspective from Theory of Constraints: "a chain is no stronger than its weakest link" [3]. Customer services are Value Streams that connect the customer to the rest of the enterprise to serve the customer. If the chain is broken anywhere, the entire customer experience suffers (more on this in Chapter 7).

What does that mean for the enterprises that are trying to survive or even thrive in the COVID-19 era, particularly those that are attempting to evolve, improve, and transform their customer experiences? Well, it means customer interactions are not optimized just by focusing on the call center or self-serving customer channel interactions. Optimizing the customer touchpoint interaction is, of course, critical. However, the customer promotion scores [4] (an objective assessment of the customer experience) will depend on the aggregation of tasks that involve multiple business units to resolve the customer request – or in other words, the Value Stream from the Customer to the rest of the enterprise.

> *Value Streams are processes that orchestrate tasks and activities involving people, enterprise applications, connected devices, and trading partners.*

iBPM is not just about technology. It is also a *management* discipline with supporting best practices and methodologies. Digital Transformation with iBPM involves four iterative intelligent methodologies [5]:

- Design Thinking Methodology
- Agile Delivery Methodology (Scrum or otherwise)
- DevOps Methodology
- Continuous Improvement Methodology

All four are about Operational Excellence.

Operational Excellence through Real-Time Lean Six Sigma

We have been – and continue to be – on the Operational Excellence path before, primarily through well-established Lean Six Sigma methodologies. Some would consider "Lean" and "Six Sigma" as passé. This is understandable as these are decades old methodologies.

The core value propositions of Lean and Six Sigma are as follows:

- *Lean* – reduce waste and improve process efficiency.
- *Six Sigma* – reduce variance and improve process quality.

It is known, both from theory [6] and practice, that getting rid of waste (Lean) in internal processes enhances Six Sigma objectives. In other words, if there is less waste in the internal operations of an enterprise (Lean), the customer experience will improve in quality and consistency (Six Sigma). Six Sigma improves quality, reduces variation, and enhances customer experience.

	# of Steps	±3σ	±4σ	±5σ	±6σ
		Overall Yield vs. Sigma (Distribution Shifted ± 1.5σ)			
	1	93.32%	99.379%	99.9767%	99.99966%
	7	61.63%	95.733%	99.839%	99.9976%
	10	50.08%	93.96%	99.768%	99.9966%
	20	25.08%	88.29%	99.536%	99.9932%
	40	6.29%	77.94%	99.074%	99.9864%

Lean reduces non-value-add steps

Six Sigma improves quality of value-add steps

Source: Six Sigma Research Institute, Motorola University, Motorola, Inc.

Lean Six Sigma drives quality, speed, and cost simultaneously

No other methodology or approach for reducing waste and improving quality has replaced Lean Six Sigma (LSS).

However, now the objectives of LSS can be achieved in real-time. "Real-Time" [7] means improvement is realized while doing the work in automated processes. The iBPM platform, methodologies, and Competency Center (covered in Chapter 10) best practices become the enablers for achieving Lean and Six Sigma improvements in real-time. Waste is avoided in real-time and value streams in all three categories (management, mission-critical, and support) are also kept in control (i.e., reduce variance and meet the objectives) in real-time.

The emergence of Low-Code/No-Code, then, in conjunction with crucial enablers such as Robotic Process Automation, AI, and Value Stream digitization within next-generation iBPM platforms – are providing compelling incentives to realize the promise of Real-Time Lean and Six Sigma.

Value-Stream-As-A-Service

The COVID-19 era highlighted the importance of collaboration between manufacturers, healthcare providers, emergency services, and governments at all levels including local, state, and national (or federal). Inter-Enterprise partnership, then, is vital.

Now, Cloud usage is increasing in the COVID-19 era. Cloud is a critical Digital Transformation enabler, and most organizations already had Cloud migration strategies prior to the pandemic. COVID-19 is accelerating Cloud migration.

Today, there are a multitude of Cloud service and Cloud computing providers. The top leaders are AWS, Microsoft Azure, and Google Cloud. The services are described as "XaaS" – where "X" can be Infrastructure, Platform, Software, or other: "aaS" of course, is "As a Service" – the essence of being provisioned on the Cloud.

- *Software as a Service (SaaS)* is perhaps the most popular type of service on the Cloud. Here, full-service business solutions are accessed on the Cloud by clients using both Web browsers and mobile devices such as tablets or smartphones. The Cloud has become a common delivery mechanism for many applications for the purpose of collaboration, content management, accounting, human resource management, and customer relationship management.

- Value-Stream-As-A-Service (VSaaS) [8] is a new model for collaboration involving multiple enterprises or business units. Each Enterprise or its specific business unit will bring the required capability. They can come in to either participate or opt-out. VSaaS supports capability "plug-ins" as participants in collaborative Value Streams. Thus, VSaaS supports collaborations between various capabilities of businesses across multiple enterprises. Here are three compelling dimensions of how COVID-19 compels and accelerates the VSaaS model [9]:

  - *Service Provider plug-ins*: the post-COVID-19 world will be an era of accelerated collaboration that will also enable various participants in VSaaS to establish credibility - Know Your Partner - and participate in the end-to-end value stream. The plug-in service providers will be leveraging technologies [10] such as Blockchain, IoT, and

Automation with continuous data mining, process mining [11], automation, and execution.

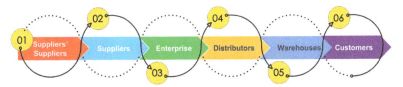

- *Agility in Manufacturing and Supplying critical parts*: There are many sources for potential disruptions to the Supply Chain – including the current pandemic. VSaaS can be automated and deployed to provide benefits that precisely target the challenges of interrupted supplies: Just-In-Time (JIT) Inventory Management, Just-Needed-Visibility, Just-Desired Innovation, Just-Required Collaboration, and Just-Predicted Mitigation of Risk.

- *Flexibility In Currency Exchanges and Decentralized Blockchain Traceability*: Blockchain will become an increasingly powerful enabler for COVID-19 VSaaS solutions. After all, it is the foundation of cryptocurrencies such as Bitcoin. Blockchains can support inter-Enterprise Masted Data Management [12]. Due to the COVID-19 recession, many countries will face a potential depreciation of their currencies. Cryptocurrencies, then, could be a potentially safer haven [13] in these difficult times.

The following image illustrates the end-to-end value stream collaboration of multiple participants in end-to-end healthcare applications. These participants include healthcare providers, emergency services, payers, hospitals, and patients – all leveraging connected devices [14].

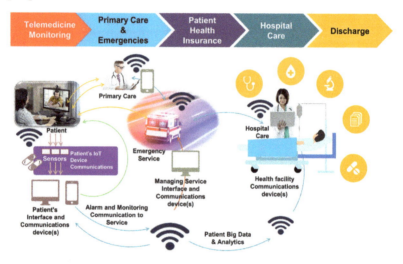

Whether it is used for patient wellness, telehealth, or for emergency life-threatening scenarios – the end-to-end health value stream involves multiple parties. With VSaaS, any of the participating entities, namely Provider, Payer, Emergency, Patient – can plug in and cooperate. The coordination and cooperation for specific patient healthcare objectives are critical in the post-COVID-19 era. The patient, as well as the other participants, are increasingly leveraging connected healthcare devices – that also become part of the end-to-end value stream as described above.

Recommendations

Although enterprises have attempted to transform themselves, many of their efforts have been in vain – especially when it comes to achieving the appropriate velocity of innovation and change. Enterprises, then, are tasked with a great need for innovation with customer experiences while at the same time, optimizing their Operational Excellence. Therefore, in addition to being responsive to the increasingly demanding digital customer, the Enterprise needs to incorporate innovations in its end-to-end value streams.

> *An enterprise is an aggregation of value streams.*

But these value streams are not static. The Enterprise needs to be *in-motion* [15]: constantly improving its Operational Excellence through changing and adapting the value streams. Behind each customer request, customer interaction, or customer dispute – there are value streams that necessarily involve multiple business units. The customer touchpoint extends to the Enterprise.

There are two complementary perspectives for Operational Excellence: best practices for internal operations through digitizing value streams, and best practices involving *value streams with trading partners* – which is at a critical point in the post-COVID-19 era. Here are the recommendations:

- *Think Big, Start Small, and Adjust:* When it comes to operational Excellence with emerging iBPM technologies and best practices, the starting point should be prioritization with the central question being: which are the low hanging fruits? There are robust techniques [16] that create the prioritized backlog of projects, thinking big, starting small, and continuously adjusting as priorities change. In the post-COVID-19 era, priorities will change!

- *Analyze and Re-Engineer Existing Processes:* Process Mining is an excellent place to start, as it will indeed expose where your bottlenecks are and provide you the opportunity to either improve, enhance, and/or automate where it makes sense.

- *Measure, Measure, and Measure and then improve,* (did I mention "Measure?"): One of the biggest advantages of Real-Time Lean Six Sigma with iBPM is that the "Measure" phase of process improvement comes entirely for free. You can align your Critical To "X" measures (where "X" can be Quality, Cost, Compliance, Revenue, Customer Experience, or anything else) in real-time. Process Improvement as a priority: Real-Time Lean Six Sigma.

- *VSaaS Ecosystem:* COVID-19 is compelling organizations to seek more dynamic partnerships.

VSaaS is an excellent approach to both allow partners to be ratified and then plug in their services in the end-to-end Value Stream such as Supply Chain. Technologies such as IoT and Blockchain, as well as AI, will be great enablers for the end-to-end solutions. VSaaS is the next phase in the evolution of the Cloud.

In the COVID-19 era, being an enterprise in motion is a must!

References

[1]   https://www.mckinsey.com/business-functions/organization/our-insights/an-operating-model-for-the-next-normal-lessons-from-agile-organizations-in-the-crisis

[2]   https://en.wikipedia.org/wiki/Business_process_re-engineering

[3]   https://www.leanproduction.com/theory-of-constraints.html

[4]   http://netpromotersystem.com/index.aspx

[5]   https://www.rtinsights.com/four-intelligent-automation-methodologies-one-objective/

[6]   http://www.sixsigmainstitute.com/leansigma/index_leansigma.shtml

[7]   https://www.linkedin.com/pulse/digital-transformation-iot-real-time-lean-six-sigma-setrag-khoshafian/

[8]   https://www.rtinsights.com/defining-the-emerging-value-stream-as-a-service-world/

[9]   https://www.linkedin.com/pulse/value-stream-as-a-service-covid-19-era-dr-setrag-khoshafian/

[10]   https://www.rtinsights.com/blockchain-iot-edge-and-vsaas-empower-autonomic-enterprises/

[11]   http://pminaction.de/home/

[12]   https://www.rtinsights.com/blockchain-for-master-data-management/

[13]   https://www.prnewswire.com/news-releases/why-cryptocurrency-could-be-a-safe-haven-during-current-health-and-economic-crisis-301084097.html

[14]   https://theiotmagazine.com/digital-transformation-of-healthcare-iomt-connectivity-ai-and-value-streams-62edc0f2be1a

[15]   https://www.rtinsights.com/what-is-the-enterprise-in-motion/

[16]   https://www.rtinsights.com/dpa-prioritization-design-thinking/

Chapter 3: Automation

The COVID-19 pandemic has pushed many enterprises to accelerate their digital transformation and modernization initiatives, especially through Automation. It is true that pre-COVID-19, there had already been developments in *work* automation that were transforming the workforce. Post-COVID-19, however, the labor world will look quite different. Those Enterprises that have their rigid structures entrenched into their foundation will not survive without necessary Automation changes. What are these changes and what is the scope of Automation impacting the workforce?

Impact of COVID-19 on Automation

A 2017 study of Automation [1] indicated that the push toward Automation threatens 800 million jobs and that one third of workers will need to learn new skills by 2030 in order to remain valuable in the job market. Another study [2] elucidated the advantages of Automation: reducing waste, eliminating human errors, and according to some workers – removing six or more hours of repetitive work on average.

McKinsey [3] estimates that 57 million US jobs, and 59 million European jobs are at risk due to the COVID-19 pandemic and its associated lockdowns. Add to that automation risks, and what you get is a double whammy! Here is how they describe it: "We find significant overlap between the workers who are vulnerable in the current downturn and those who hold jobs susceptible to Automation [4] in the future. In addition to the effects of technology, the crisis itself may create lasting changes in consumer behavior and health protocols. To put vulnerable workers on more promising and sustainable paths, the US response should incorporate a longer-term view about the resulting occupational shifts and the development of skills." As we shall see in the *Recommendations* section below, the current crises which will continue to impact us for many years to come, could indeed prove to be an excellent opportunity!

The Spectrum of Automation in the COVID-19 Era

There is a spectrum of work and worker types when it comes to Automation – as illustrated here. With COVID-19, what we are starting to witness is a significant shift toward more automation as well as increased involvement of cognitive workers – directly reflected in the workforce. Automation has the capacity to reduce the most mundane tasks and is certainly being used for this purpose, but more surprisingly it is even being used for some not-so-mundane tasks. All industry sectors have been impacted. This, of course, implies the loss

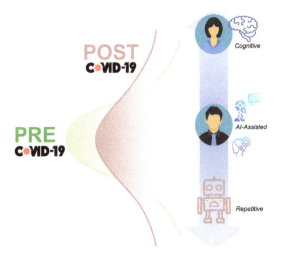

of jobs across many of these sectors and industries. As discussed in Chapter One, there are also cultural shifts due to virtualization that are impacting work automation, especially in customer services.

- *Repetitive Work* - Automated through Robots and Robotic Automation: Increasingly, robots are replacing routine and repetitive manual work. This comprises the "long tail" of tasks that are allocated to relatively low paying repetitive jobs, managed by the business. These jobs are now increasingly automated with robots – including actual physical robots that can, for instance, operate a warehouse by moving boxes around, or clean the floor in large plants – and of course, you have extensive robotics in Manufacturing. We can also have software robots. Repetitive desktop tasks, for instance, could be automated through robotic software automation—which would save a considerable amount of time while avoiding potential human errors. COVID-19 is causing a sharp increase in Automation across all sectors.

- *AI-Assisted Work*: Now, for tasks that are more mission-critical and provide a higher business value (and typically higher transaction volume), there are AI-assisted workers that are guided by increasingly intelligent software that leverages business rules, analytics, and machine learning. It is akin to having a smart Siri or Alexa, aiding the worker in the completion of their tasks. What we are witnessing more and more is that workers are being assisted by bots and Intelligent Virtual Assistants (IVAs) with increasingly sophisticated Natural Language Processing capabilities, combined with the appropriate contextual knowledge for the task or interaction at hand. Most organizations reduced staffing for customer service during COVID-19. Organizations have increasingly turned toward bots + IVAs to make the initial identification of customer issues and *then* involve a human agent - assisting the human agent to resolve the customer issue.

- *Cognitive Work*: Cognitive workers are experts. We saw a sharp rise in telehealth and virtual visits in the healthcare sector. The expert doctors and nurses are the irreplaceable cognitive workers par excellence, as are the healthcare payers and providers. Telehealth [5] witnessed a substantial increase in the initial stages of the pandemic, which has leveled off. All industry sectors are experiencing both remote work with AI-assisted Automation and involvement of cognitive workers who are exceptionally good at

providing expertise and dealing with exceptions. No "Artificial" intelligence will be able to replace these valued cognitive workers or the nuances of their experience. The human touch, human experience, and involvement, are even more critical in the post-COVID-19 era. The knowledge and know-how of this vital category of workers need to be harvested and digitized. That will take time and it will not be 100%. Ideally, they need to work closely with data scientists – to complement human knowledge with data and machine discovered models. Most importantly, their experience needs to be harvested and digitized in the context of end-to-end value streams.

Industry 4.0 in the post-COVID-19 era

In Process as well as Discrete Manufacturing – even before the pandemic – manufacturers were introducing Automation and increasingly sophisticated robotics and edge computing in all phases of manufacturing. With COVID-19, Robotics and Automation are becoming even more critical in Manufacturing – especially discrete Manufacturing, which has evolved to Industry 4.0. The manufacturing industry – especially automotive original equipment manufacturers (OEMs) – were in a significant digital transition, and COVID-19 accelerated and increased Automation, Analytics, and the Cloud primarily. The Fourth Industrial Revolution in Manufacturing is in full swing. IoT, AI and Robotics Automation are revolutionizing Manufacturing end-to-end - sometimes with noticeable variances in spending on Industry 4.0

technologies [6]. The impact of Automation and Robotics with IoT connectivity extends beyond the shop floor.

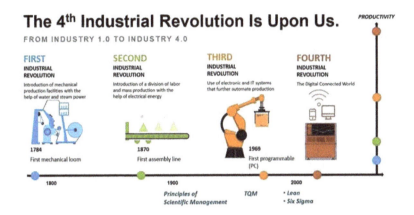

The 4ᵗʰ Industrial Revolution Is Upon Us.

FROM INDUSTRY 1.0 TO INDUSTRY 4.0

The Automation and connectivity of manufactured devices for vehicles or automotive fleets are disrupting relationship dynamics between manufacturers, dealers, suppliers, service organizations, and – most importantly – consumers. In the emerging era of Industry 4.0 and smart Manufacturing, the value streams from manufacturing to *aftermarket services* are radically transformed.

The connectivity of manufacturers to customers, and specifically for automotive OEMs, is shifting to a much closer, more monitored, and responsive relationship. Plus, in Process Manufacturing, we are witnessing the increased deployment of automated and semi-automated drones and robots. Intelligence and Automation are also increasingly deployed at the *edges* – which often alleviates the need for human interventions or contact: again, a critical trend that was already in play but has certainly become quite crucial post-COVID-19.

Warehouse and Supply Chain Management, which is critical in many industries, showed serious vulnerabilities during the pandemic. We are starting to see movement to optimize and change through Automation, and diversity of sourcing [7]. However, increased pressure on workers – particularly for supplies that are in high demand or supply that is frequently ordered in small quantities – in conjunction with concerns over the safety of the workers, has become a fertile ground for Automation for warehouses and supply chain in general. While there were already nascent trends toward Automation, COVID-19 accelerated the utilization of robots for a variety of purposes in warehouses: packaging, scanning, moving boxes, cleaning floors, and identifying items – to name a few.

Driving the Enterprise-in-Motion with Hyperautomation

Automation is the engine that powers and moves the Enterprise-in-Motion [8]. Even before COVID-19 in the year of 2019, Gartner had identified "*hyperautomation*" as the number one trend in 2020 [9]. Specifically, it "deals with the application of advanced technologies, including artificial intelligence (AI) and machine learning (ML), to increasingly automate processes and augment humans. Hyperautomation extends across a range of tools that can be automated, but also refers to the sophistication of the Automation."

Robotic Process Automation (RPA) [10] – especially for repetitive tasks in the front or back office – is a powerful enabler for hyperautomation. The same is true with AI for intelligent and virtual assistants.

Instead of human workers (e.g., agents or customer service representatives) accessing various applications on their desktops, copying information between various screens, or traversing a plethora of legacy applications, the RPA software robot can instead automatically achieve the same repetitive tasks, at a much faster rate and with far fewer errors. The software robot does the work: changing the address of the customer in multiple applications, processing invoices copying data from one account and reconciling it in another - and so on.

There are also other background process applications of RPA: where the automated software robot wakes up and reconciles the data in various data repositories, applications, or databases in the background.

However, before deploying an RPA solution, organizations realize they need first to identify automation opportunities within their operations and then automate these repetitive tasks or introduce intelligent agents of Automation. Operational Excellence experts know that automating bad processes could make matters even worse. After all, RPA is no panacea. The following two rules on technology from Bill Gates [11] are spot-on: "The first rule of any technology used in a business is that Automation applied to an efficient operation will magnify the efficiency. The second is that Automation applied to an inefficient operation will magnify the inefficiency." Spot on!

Enter Process Mining [12].

Briefly, through process mining, an organization can analyze the transaction logs of their systems of record and mine them for insights and optimization opportunities. Process mining, followed by careful analysis for operational efficiency, should always precede any deployment or execution efforts with RPA or intelligent Business Process Management (iBPM). Process mining discovers process maps and all their variations from the transactional data logs. It is not a good idea, in that case, to automate bad processes. Understanding the quality of processes needs careful analysis – so this becomes a necessary step and enabler for successful RPA. Process Mining can provide intelligent analysis of the *as-is* processes by clarifying the bottlenecks and the many variances of the process. Then the operational excellence analysts can highlight the needed opportunities through Automation – especially RPA.

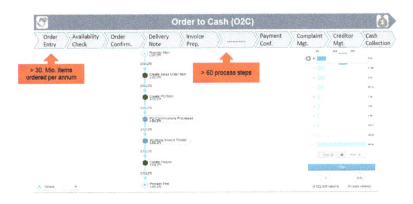

The Siemens Order to Cache (O2C) process improvement with process mining is a compelling case study. It is highlighted here [13] and in more detail in Chapter 9 of Process Mining in Action [14]. The key performance improvement objective is the average number of manual touches required for the order. This process has 60 steps and 30 million activities per year. In fact, there are more than 900,000 variations of the process! After the analysis and identification of opportunities, the operational excellence results were promising: a higher rate of Automation by 24%, an 11% reduction in rework, and 10 million fewer manual touches a year.

Automation Strategy (AS)

Enterprises of all sizes generate an enormous amount of data, and there are typically several types of silos that cause a considerable amount of waste.

Enterprises involve many siloed systems of record. The data is aggregated in a plethora of SQL and NoSQL intelligent databases [15]. Various patterns are subsequently detected through data mining and process mining. The business logic and process models are then analyzed within an overall Automation Strategy. The low hanging fruits – which are generally processes with high value and potential for automation optimization – can then be operationalized in end-to-end Process Automation solutions. More specifically, the *Action* leverages the *Intelligence* harvested from the data or human cognitive experts and then executes them through Automated Processes.

Intelligent Process Automation enablers used for digitizing value streams which connect customers, partners, and the entire ecosystem of organizations, are all available through technologies such as Robotic Process Automation (RPA) and intelligent Business Process

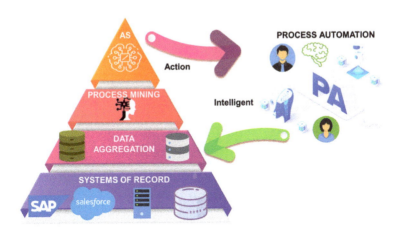

Management (iBPM) [16]. Connecting various siloes in the organizations will become critical. However, here we see again that the potential hindrances to connectivity are cultural. The ROI of Process Automation emanates from three complementary and interdependent areas:

- *Process efficiency in planning and deploying innovations*: The continuous innovation and deployment involve four Digital Transformation methodologies [17]: Design Thinking, Agile, DevOps, and Operational Excellence. It starts with prioritization [18]– thinking big for Automation but starting small with the most impactful low hanging fruits.

- *Process efficiency in automated execution*: The spectrum of Automation summarized above – from robotics to AI-assisted to cognitive worker participation – is critical for resolving manual handoffs and silos. The completion and resolution of end-to-end value streams can be optimized from days to hours with the use of process automation.

- *Process efficiency through monitoring and improvement*: Out of the box business activity dashboards, reports, and automated alerts can dynamically monitor if work is processed on time, if contractual SLAs are being met, and if processes are running optimally. These are actionable monitoring reports – where managers, for instance, can re-assign tasks from under-performers to others.

Recommendations

Automation, combined with COVID-19, is causing a crisis in the labor market – and this will only get worse. Technology will advance, and this means it will automate more. COVID-19 is having a tremendous impact on behaviors – cultural implications whose ramifications will be felt for many generations.

The post-COVID-19 era with all uncertainties is a huge opportunity for hyperautomation. Here are the top recommendations:

- *Reskill and Upskill:* Organizations need to upskill and reskill their employees. Automation is coming and its demand got accelerated post-Covid-19. Workers need to know how to process work with bots and Intelligent Virtual Assistants. Operational Excellence analysts and developers (increasingly Citizen Developers - Chapter 4) need to learn Process Mining, RPA and iBPM platforms. The unstoppable shifts are toward more Automation of repetitive work and the emergence of the cognitive worker. Both are opportunities for reskilling and upskilling.

- *Prioritization for Automation:* The most important deliverable of the ideation phase in Design Thinking methodology (Chapter 6) is Prioritization – something that is also included in Operational Excellence methodologies - such as Real-Time Lean Six Sigma (Chapter 2). Automation has a spectrum of opportunities and enterprises that embark upon the robust Automation Strategy roadmaps need to identify and continuously revise the low hanging fruits of Automation.

- *Process and Data Mining:* Be bold and analyze your as-is processes with honesty. Most enterprises understand this important area of Data Science and Data Mining – but they lack the key skills and understanding of Process Science and Process Mining. In Chapter 5 we will delve deeper into Data Science. For now, it is critical to develop Process Mining skills and deploy it as an essential component of an overall Automation Strategy initiative.

- *Entrepreneur and Startup mind frame*: Perhaps most importantly, enterprises of all sizes need to prioritize and focus on innovation opportunities. Sure, Automation is disruptive, but it is also powerful – and a robust Automation Strategy can ensure survival and growth amid the uncertainties brought about by COVID-19. Every organization needs to operate with the mentality and Culture of a startup: where enthusiasm, empowerment, and innovative thinking permeates the very DNA of the organization.

References

[1]   https://www.mckinsey.com/global-themes/future-of-organizations-and-work/what-the-future-of-work-will-mean-for-jobs-skills-and-wages

[2]   https://www.smartsheet.com/sites/default/files/smartsheet-automation-workplace.pdf

[3]   https://www.mckinsey.com/industries/public-and-social-sector/our-insights/covid-19-and-jobs-monitoring-the-us-impact-on-people-and-places

[4]   https://www.mckinsey.com/featured-insights/future-of-work/the-future-of-work-in-america-people-and-places-today-and-tomorrow

[5]   https://www.healthrecoverysolutions.com/hubfs/June%20 2020%20Research%20Articles/Telehealth%20transformation-%20 COVID-19%20and%20the%20rise%20of%20virtual%20care.pdf

[6]   https://www.hfsresearch.com/research/prepare-now-for-a-splurge-on-industry-4-0-services-after-covid-19/

[7]   https://www.weforum.org/agenda/2020/05/this-is-what-global-supply-chains-will-look-like-after-covid-19/

[8]   https://www.rtinsights.com/what-is-the-enterprise-in-motion/

[9]   https://www.gartner.com/smarterwithgartner/gartner-top-10-strategic-technology-trends-for-2020/

[10]   https://theiotmagazine.com/iot-robotics-for-the-spectrum-of-work-automation-f6e56f234fd8

[11]   https://www.optimize.me/quotes/bill-gates/20675-the-first-rule-of-any-technology-used-in/

[12]   https://en.wikipedia.org/wiki/Process_mining

[13]   https://www.healthrecoverysolutions.com/hubfs/June%20 2020%20Research%20Articles/Telehealth%20transformation-%20 COVID-19%20and%20the%20rise%20of%20virtual%20care.pdf

[14]   https://www.amazon.com/Process-Mining-Action-Principles-Outlook/dp/3030401715/

[15]   https://www.rtinsights.com/process-data-its-about-time/

[16]   https://www.amazon.com/Intelligent-BPM-Next-Wave-Customer-
        centric/dp/0986052108

[17]   https://www.rtinsights.com/four-intelligent-automation-
        methodologies-one-objective/

[18]   https://www.rtinsights.com/dpa-prioritization-design-thinking/

Chapter 4: No Code Citizen Developers

While digital transformation and modernization initiatives were starting to take hold before COVID-19 entered the scene, the post-COVID-19 era is certainly catalyzing the push for many enterprises to re-consider their current efforts—especially in accelerating the development and deployment of innovative applications. Value Stream mapping and modeling for Operational Excellence (Chapter 2) as well as automation of processes (Chapter 3) need application development—coding!

The emergence of Citizen Developers leveraging Low Code/No Code platforms has profound transformative implications both for Enterprises and Startups.

Evolution of Programming

Low Code/No Code is the next phase in the evolution of programming (also known as "coding"). The transition from assembly to high-level procedural programming (examples include C and Pascal) and then from high-level procedural languages to object orientation (examples include Java and C#) have enabled us to achieve substantial digitization and productivity gains. There are now tens of millions of developers for programming languages such as Java, C#, JavaScript, Python, and a harvest of relatively new and emerging programming languages such as Swift, Go, Kotlin, and many others. With these languages - and there are way too many - the programmer always needs to learn and write the cumbersome text of the Code and debug it. Though there are many programming languages, they all share this core inefficiency. Traditional software development then, is a clunky, slow, and error-prone process that keeps the developer and business stakeholders in their silos.

The lack of alignment between what is required by the business stakeholders and what then ends up as an application by the programmers is considerable – this factor alone has been a source of contention and frustration. The paradigm of an initial design of the programming model in an Interactive Development

Environment (IDE) and then coding via the programming language syntax has remained, by and large, *unchanged.*

The following illustrates the popularity of programming languages in 2020 [1].

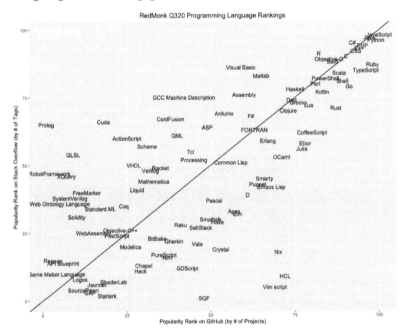

When looking at this ranking – and many other analyses of popular programming languages – one gets the distinct impression that this is all there is when it comes to "programming" and developing applications in different domains. Universities and even high schools teach programming for one or more of these languages.

What is interesting is that Low Code/No Code is completely missing in programming language rankings. They are, of course, different than *conventional* programming languages. But they achieve the same objectives: developing and deploying scalable applications while supporting computational-complete constructs, with easy to use drag and drop interfaces. Even their designated name "No" Code or at least "Low" code is telling. How can programming be done without code?

> *We are now witnessing the emergence of Low Code/No Code as a programming paradigm that provides tremendous productivity advantages, which is critical in the post-COVID-19 era.*

As the name suggests, Low Code/No Code platforms enable the development of applications with little to no "coding." The delineations between Low Code and No Code are somewhat blurred, and they are only getting murkier. But briefly, No Code targets business stakeholders (aka Citizen Developers) and subject-matter experts (also Citizen Developers) who can build business applications with no coding – just using drag and drop, easy to use constructs. Low Code involves some coding and is generally associated with the productivity of technical developers or programmers.

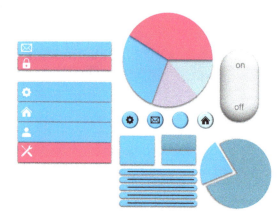

> *Low Code/No Code uses easy to use widgets, forms, and other user interface constructs to easily build solutions - even by business users who are not familiar with coding.*

Low Code/No Code, then, is transformational in the world of programming. It is also essential in the post-COVID-19 era for both enterprises and startups. Organizations need to develop an *antifragile* disposition, continually adjusting as the world around them changes and evolves. They need to emulate the behavior of enterprises and startups in-motion [2]. Low Code/No Code platforms are a tremendous enabler for agility.

Forrester [3] predicts that Low Code will grow at 40% and become a $21.2 Billion market by 2022. According to Gartner [4], 65% of applications will be developed from Low Code by 2024. Although low Code/No Code is not "hype" or a momentary interest, it is also no panacea. It does entail its own unique challenges, but it is revolutionary and is accelerating the pace of innovation for both enterprises and startups.

The achievements in the advances of programming languages pale in comparison to the productivity gains one could realize when developing applications with Low Code/No Code. It enables robust, fast, and efficient development of applications in all categories. I was involved in a comparative productivity benchmark test between traditional development (using Java) and a model-driven Low Code/No Code development project.

The results were impressive: 5X to 7X productivity [5] improvement with Low Code/No Code model-driven development. A survey by No-Code Census in 2020 showed a 4.6X productivity gain [6] over traditional programming. Even a modest 50% - 75% improvement is still very much a formidable gain.

Both internal applications and customer-facing applications can be built with Low Code/No Code. For Startups, Low Code/No Code can achieve accelerated development of Minimum Viable Products [7] (MVPs). For established Enterprises, Low Code/No Code can help accelerate Digital Transformation initiatives toward the needed digital modernization and change.

Citizen Developers

Despite the many advances in productivity tools, methodologies, and techniques, most organizations still suffer from Business-Technical Developers-Operations silos. Although Low Code/No Code does have challenges, it is accelerating innovations for both enterprises and startups. This is because it provides a common inter-silo "language" for the different functional units within the organization.

Low Code/No Code is not so much about the tooling but more about functioning as an enabler for the Culture (Chapter 1 and Chapter 6) of innovation and digital transformation – which is a cultural shift to empower the business stakeholder and obliterate silos.

The anti-fragile and anti-silo transformation are critical in the post-COVID-19 era.

> *Low Code/No Code is empowering "Citizen Developers" all over the world.*

But who exactly are these Citizen Developers? Hint: it's you. Founders in startups, Business stakeholders in Enterprises, Operations subject-matter experts, and yes, conventional programmers are *Citizen Developers* that benefit tremendously from the possibilities of Low Code/ No Code. The new generation of application development environments is getting much easier to use, allowing anyone –most notably the younger and more tech-savvy generations – to build small and robust enterprise applications.

Citizen Developer stakeholders and subject-matter experts can be involved in all phases and iterations of robust and continuously improving methodologies.

Citizen Developers are crucial in prioritizing MVPs or applications, the development of the MVP, the productization of the application, monitoring, and continuously improving. For instance, a founder in a startup can prioritize and build an MVP (typically in collaboration with other participants). They can be involved in designing the structure of the database, defining business logic for constraints or approvals, or enhancing the UI in the development iterations. Post-deployment, subject matter experts can assess the performance as well as the functionality of the application and introduce additional business logic themselves – all these "programming" or "coding" tasks – as *Citizen Developers*. The governance and methodology best practices for Low Code/No Code are therefore critical. There will typically be a learning curve for selected Low Code/No Code platforms.

Low Code/No Code Platforms

Low Code/No Code is a revolution. Low Code/No Code enables robust, fast, and efficient development of applications across all major categories: Web, Mobile, Enterprise, and others. These Low Code/No Code platforms can also be leveraged for internal as well as customer-facing application development. Low Code/ No Code platforms do have their specific underlying conventions and core models. So, there is a learning curve – it will not be easy from the get-go. However, once the various stakeholders master the tool, the gains in productivity will be considerable.

There are many styles and types of Low Code/No Code platforms. Some of these have evolved from predecessor model-driven platforms that have attempted to introduce interactive and easy to use drag and drop features. As summarized here [8], the following is a partial list of different styles and options of Low Code/No Code platforms:

- *Web site low-code/no-code platforms*: Enterprises of all sizes can leverage these platforms: e.g., WebFlow.
- *Database management low-code/no-code platforms*: On the high end (enterprise), you have platforms such as Airtable.
- *Automated integration low-code/no-code platforms*: There are several exciting and emerging platforms such as Zapier and Integromat.
- *Mobile application development*: Most low-code/no-code platforms, such as Bubble, provide responsive UI capabilities for mobile applications. Others such as Thunkable offer native support for the leading mobile operations systems (iOS and Android).

There are other more specialized categories such as:

- *E-commerce and online stores*: A leading example in this category is Shopify.
- *Work management*: An excellent example in this category is Monday.com.

- **ERP applications**: An interesting example is Zoho. Another significant and impactful platform for ERP and CRM is Salesforce.
- **Blockchain:** Atra is an example in this category for building No Code/Low Code decentralized applications.
- **IoT**: Cumulocity from Software AG is an example of a Low Code Industrial IoT platform.
- **Artificial intelligence**: A fascinating area for low-code/no-code is AI, and we are now starting to see the emergence of tools in this area. An example here is C3 AI Ex Machina.

Model-driven [9] development platforms – especially in the Business Process Management category – were the Low Code/No Code predecessors. BPM evolved to intelligent Business Process Management (iBPM), with more drag and drop easy to use User Interfaces (UI): supporting Low Code/No Code process-centric application development – primarily for operational excellence and automated value streams.

The spectrum of Low Code/No Code platforms involves incumbents, especially from iBPM, that have incorporated additional capabilities to target Citizen Developers. But what is perhaps even more exciting is that there is a new harvest of impressive and easy-to-use Low Code/No Code platforms that could potentially provide disruptions to the Low Code/No Code ecosystem as it currently stands. One of these – and there are many – for Web application development is Bubble.io [10]. In addition to the database

– with built-in User type – and integration capabilities, Bubble.io has a marketplace of free and for-purchase affordable templates from third parties that can be easily customized. There is also a rich collection of plugins to integrate with; for instance, collaboration platforms such as Slack. The following illustrates a free template for cryptocurrencies that can easily be customized in its UI, business logic, or database.

Recommendations

The Low Code/No Code platform and solution market are fragmented and confusing. There are enterprise Low Code platforms and those that are more applicable to medium-sized and smaller enterprises. Of course, it is a spectrum, and the delineations are not that sharp. Often listings in one category (e.g., Enterprise Low Code) do not mention platforms in the other (e.g., No Code for small to medium-sized businesses). There are definite challenges for Low Code/No Code platforms [8].

Yet, they provide tremendous advantages when developing and deploying innovative applications. The speed of development could be existential – especially in the post-COVID-19 era.

Here are the top recommendations for Low Code/No Code:

• *Platform Selection – balancing capability with cost*: The current range of Low Code/No Code platforms on the market today is impressive. It is also fragmented and confusing. There are taxonomies and reports – but typically, they do not cover all the platforms. It is most likely that multiple Low Code/No Code platforms will be needed to produce an innovative application. Pricing and total cost of ownership will also be critical – as some of the platforms are quite expensive. As noted above, there are different types (process-centric, Web App, database-centric, mobile-centric, etc.) of Low Code/No Code platforms that must be carefully analyzed.

• *Reskill and Upskill for Low Code/No Code*: Organizations need to leverage the lockdown and the resulting gain in time due to work-from-home directives to upskill and reskill their employees in selected and Low Code/No Code platforms. Each platform entails a necessary learning curve: some are more difficult than others; some platforms have robust development, education, and support communities. The innovation team needs to consider all this and other dimensions of Low Code/ No Code.

- *Citizen Developer Culture:* This is extremely important. Some business stakeholders in enterprises or founders in startups might be reluctant to get involved in "development" as it is perceived to be cumbersome. However, a new generation of tech-savvy workers is entering the workforce. At the same time, the new generation of Low Code/No Code application development environments are becoming much easier to use – allowing Citizen Developers to build or collaborate in creating robust, innovative applications.

- *Design Sprints* – being lean and effective: Check the following article [11] on the Sprint methodology [12]. There is a perfect fit either during or immediately post the 4–5-day methodology to leverage Low Code/ No Code for a Minimum Viable Product (MVP). The end-user testing can, and most likely *will*, end up with enhancements that could be easily and speedily achieved with a Low Code/No Code platform.

Low-code/no-code is no panacea. It has several challenges as summarized here [8]:

- There Is a learning curve for any No Code/Low Code platform.
- Pricing - especially for the enterprise Low Code platforms - can be steep or confusing.

- The communities and resources are not as robust - compared to conventional programming languages.
- Potentially multiple tools or Low Code/No Code platforms might be needed for the same Web or mobile applications.

There are others. However, despite these challenges, Low Code/No Code empowering Citizen Developers remains a formidable trend for alleviating Digital Transformation Debt with innovative solutions both for incumbent enterprises and startups.

References

[1]   https://redmonk.com/kfitzpatrick/2020/07/29/redmonk-slackchat-june-2020-programming-language-rankings/

[2]   https://www.rtinsights.com/what-is-the-enterprise-in-motion/

[3]   https://www.techadv.com/blog/rise-low-code-2020-and-beyond

[4]   https://www.gartner.com/doc/reprints?ct=190711&id=1-1FKNU1TK

[5]   https://www.capgemini.com/wp-content/uploads/2017/07/b_SmartBPM_vs._Eclipse_IDE.pdf

[6]   https://nocodecensus.com/

[7]   https://www.startupassistant.io/blog/no-codelow-code-mvps

[8]   https://venturebeat.com/2021/02/14/no-code-low-code-why-you-should-be-paying-attention/

[9]   https://books.google.com/books/about/Intelligent_BPM.html?id=IYACnwEACAAJ

[10]   https://bubble.io/

[11]   https://www.linkedin.com/pulse/going-lean-during-quarantine-dr-setrag-khoshafian/

[12]   https://www.amazon.com/Sprint-Solve-Problems-Test-Ideas/dp/150112174X/

Chapter 5: Citizen Data Scientists

Post-COVID-19, Enterprises need to understand the trends embedded in enterprise, sensor, customer, and partner *Data*. Digitization of value streams for operational excellence (Chapter 2) and the hyperautomation (Chapter 3) of the enterprise with empowered Citizen Developers (Chapter 4) needs to be complemented with the operationalization through Citizen *Data Scientist*. All working toward an in motion and autonomic [1] Enterprise to alleviate Digital Transformation Debt.

Data-Centric Organization

By any estimate, the digital era is facing an unprecedented explosion of information or Digital Data! Digital technologies, solutions, and content generate 2.5 quintillion bytes of data [2] each day!

Organizations are hoarding data. But quite often, mining and benefiting from the heterogeneous data lakes is difficult. Storing data is one thing. Benefiting from it, quite a different challenge. Fortunately, a new harvest of productivity, self-service, drag-and-drop data tools is emerging, allowing *Citizens* (regular stakeholders - as indicated in Chapter 4) to mine the knowledge from the Data. This entails deploying robust Data Science analytical tools for machine learning, or even deep learning models that can benefit (aka "monetize") from the Data.

> *We are witnessing the emergence of easy-to-use Citizen AI tools for customer engagement [3], with proven results. These are nothing short of Artificial Intelligence platforms for the masses.*

It is evident that in the post-COVID-19 era, Data is becoming even more critical. The application of the models mined from the COVID-19 infection databases is an obvious example. Equally important are the supply chain, societal interaction, and overall economic trends amid shifts and transformation. The COVID-19 era is also accelerating the "Process + Data" [4] narrative, where organizations need to complement and balance data-centricity (this Chapter 5) combined with the digitization and Automation of value streams (Chapter 2 and 3). The bottom line is, whether pre- or post-COVID-19: *it is not just about the data*. The insights need to be mined, discovered, or harvested from the vast, often convoluted lakes of data. Raw data to insights, then, should be the mantra. Finally, once insights are discovered, they need to be *acted upon*.

Database Management Systems (DBMS)

DBMSs that separate the management of the data from the application first appeared on the scene in the 1970s with navigational hierarchical and network models. In the 1980s, we saw a significant evolution to relational databases [5] that became pretty popular, particularly with SQL's emergence as the de-facto query language for databases! The evolution of databases from relational

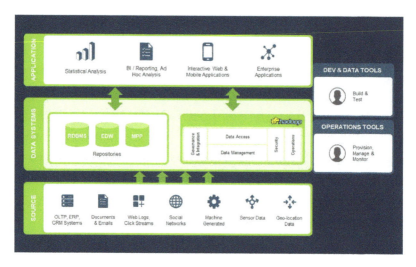

included Object-Oriented Databases [6] that combined Object-Oriented and Database capabilities for persistent storage of objects and Object-Relational Databases [7] that combine the characteristics of both relational and object-oriented databases.

More recently, particularly when handling large unstructured multi-media data in new digital applications, we saw the emergence of NoSQL [8] to handle the demands of Big Data [9]: with large volume, variety, velocity, and veracity. This new generation of databases focuses on dealing with the explosion of heterogeneous data and the storage and management of this Data for innovative Internet applications (especially IoT). By and large, most transactional data for mission-critical systems of record (which require transactional integrity) remain relational, with all these trends culminating in *intelligent DBMSs.*

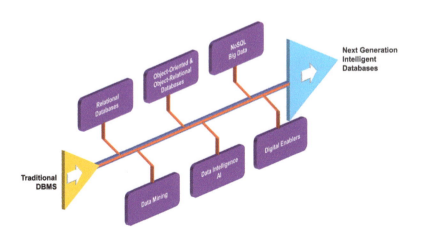

Data Lakes

Recently we have also seen the emergence of "Data Lakes." Here is how AWS [10] explains "Data Lakes:"

> *Faced with massive volumes and heterogeneous types of data, organizations are finding that in order to deliver insights in a timely manner, they need a data storage and analytics solution that offers more agility and flexibility than traditional data management systems... Data Lake allows an organization to store all their data, structured and unstructured, in one, centralized repository.*

The following illustrates the key components and capabilities of a Data Lake [11].

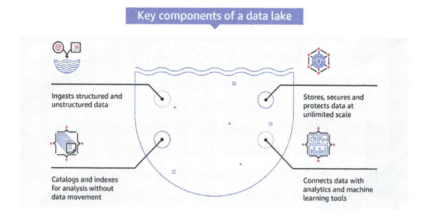

The emergence of many heterogeneous data sources is at the core of the Data Lake. A robust Data Lake strategic implementation ingests heterogeneous data from different sources, stores and secures them, and integrates the Data with AI tools.

The Data Scientist

The sections above illustrate the complexity of Data in enterprises – there are too many databases, repositories, sources, and strategies. The Data is structured (as in Relational Databases) and Unstructured for multi-media Data typically managed by NoSQL databases. Data Lakes aggregate and ingest the heterogeneous Data. To become an effective Data-centric organization, we have seen the emergence of a new role: The Data Scientist.

Why the new role? Many assumptions that we had taken for granted in the management of databases, including the integrity or logic of the independence of the data from the application, are now being challenged. The past couple of decades have engendered powerful gatekeepers of the enterprise data (the Database Administrators (DBA)) [12] who at times block the agility and speed of change needed to sustain business requirements. The world – or I should say the digital world – is changing. The introduction of NoSQL databases [13], especially for Big Data [14], has introduced additional complexity for managing and maintaining heterogeneous DBMSs' consistency. This transformational change emanates solely from the need to engage customers directly. Yet, it also results from the explosion of information on the Internet, especially with the Internet of Things [15].

More importantly, however, the mining of business value through analysis and machine learning techniques has given rise to this new – and sometimes DBA evolved role in the enterprise, namely the "Data Scientist."

Here is a good definition of the role of a Data Scientist from a business perspective [16]:

> *A data scientist conducts many important functions: identifying important questions, collecting relevant data from various sources, stores and organizes data, deciphering useful information, and finally translating it into business solutions and then communicating the findings to affect the business positively.*

Data Science involves many disciplines. Data Scientists, then, need to possess many important skills – from mathematics, statistics, and machine learning, to programming and more. Perhaps more importantly, Data Scientists need to communicate and present their findings in clear terms that the business will understand. Additionally, they need to be subject matter experts and creative—one role for all this spectrum. It is certainly no wonder Data Scientists are in great demand! Here is a great illustration [17] of Data Science:

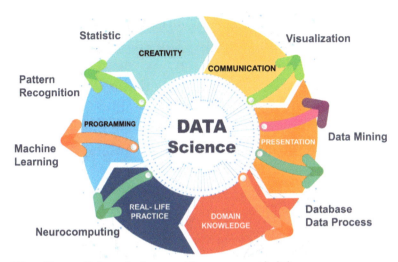

The Data Scientist's continuous activities occur across three fundamental areas: Data Analysis, Programming, and Business Analysis for concrete business results. Unfortunately, poor data quality complicates the Data Scientist's tasks and objectives. About 70% of their effort is to ingest, prepare, and cleanse data.

In my interactions with Data Scientists, they sometimes object to this estimate, stating that it is more. In other words, only 10% - 30% of their time is the discovery of meaningful insights and business value from the often unruly and heterogeneous data sets!

The Citizen Data Scientist

As indicated above, Data Science involves many distinct disciplines. Gartner [18] defines "citizen data scientist as a person who creates or generates models that use advanced diagnostic analytics or predictive and prescriptive capabilities, but whose primary job function is outside the field of statistics and analytics." The 2017 article [19] predicts 40% of Data Science tasks will be automated by 2020. This is a striking figure. Well, in 2021, we are not even close to that level of Automation. Still, Data Scientists spend a majority of their time cleaning and preparing the analysis and discovery data.

> *Can we have Citizen Data Scientists - as we have Citizen Developers?*

The trend toward empowered Citizens who can achieve Data Science objectives is not just hype. However, it has a long way to go. The good news is that some emerging tools and platforms are addressing the requirements of Data Scientists.

Here are some productivity, intelligence, and automation technologies that support Citizen Data Scientists:

- *Automation of Data Preparation*: This is the most crucial category, like cleaning and preparing the data constitutes more than 70% of the Data Scientists' effort. We are starting to see some tools addressing these needs. Tableau Prep [20], for example, "... changes the way traditional data prep is performed in an organization. By providing a visual and direct way to combine, shape, and clean data, Tableau Prep makes it easier for analysts and business users to start their analysis, faster."

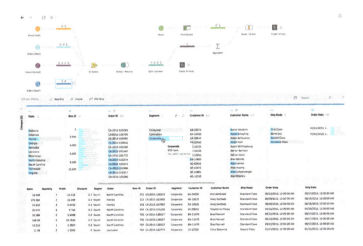

- *Low Code/No Code Data Integration*: Several emerging and robust tools exist to automate data integration and aggregation from different sources. Most structured and unstructured databases have Application Programming Interfaces (APIs). These productivity and automation tools provide easy-to-use drag and drop capabilities for Data integration. Parabola [21] is an example of a Low Code/No Code platform for automating integration.

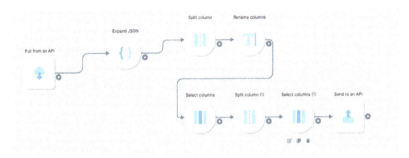

- *Automating Machine Learning (AutoML)*: Automation in data integration and preparation is a pre-requisite for analysis and machine learning. Machine Learning leverages Artificial Intelligence (AI) algorithms to discover patterns in the data. This is critical in the overall Data Science process. Now, when we shift to Citizen Data Scientists, it becomes critical to automate machine learning. Here is one definition of AutoML [22] – which is a bit extreme but drives home the objective of AutoML: "Automated machine learning, or AutoML, aims to reduce or eliminate the need for skilled data scientists to build machine learning and deep learning models. Instead, an AutoML system allows you to provide the labeled training data as input and receive an optimized model as output." Several vendors are positioning their advanced AI automation tools as AutoML – this includes Google's Cloud AutoML [23] and IBM Watson's AutoAI [24].

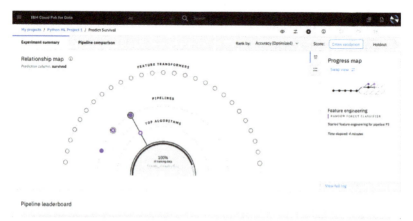

- *End-To-End Citizen Data Science Tools*: As described earlier, multi-discipline Data Science has many phases. The overall workflow involves data sourcing, preparation, analysis, modeling, prioritizing the models, and then deployment. One example of such a platform is DataRobot. Here is how they describe [25] their support for Citizen Data Scientists: "Citizen data scientists can upload a dataset to DataRobot and pick a target variable [26] based on the practical business problem they wish to solve. The platform automatically applies best practices for data preparation and pre-processing, feature engineering [27], and model training and validation [28]." The Wiki article [25] illustrates the end-to-end workflow for Citizen Data Scientists.

With these platforms, the dream of a Citizen Data Scientist spanning Automation and self-service with drag and drop intuitive productivity tools, is slowly becoming a reality. We still have a long way to go.

Recommendations

Data Science is complicated. The Data *Science* also has many disparate and confusing elements. Yet, they provide tremendous advantages when developing and deploying innovative applications. The speed of development could be existential in the post-COVID-19 era.

COVID-19 delivers a robust opportunity for organizations to rethink roles and tools for innovation and become a startup or an enterprise in motion. Here are the top recommendations:

- *Citizen Data Scientist Culture*: The Data-centric enterprise needs to provide strategic and pragmatic tools for Citizen Data Scientists: from Data Lakes to Visualization to No Code Development to Machine Learning. Given its complexity, this will most likely be a partnership between conventional data science technical roles, Data tools, and business savvy Citizen Data Scientists for specific data science milestones.

- *Data Cleansing and Preparation Automation*: The first place to start with Automation and self-service Data Science is the data cleansing and preparation phase, which typically consumes 70%+ of the Data Scientists' efforts. Given the heterogeneous nature of these data sources, it is quite a complex operation. However, it is critical for success. This typically requires a partnership between technical Data Scientists and Citizen Data Scientists – with most of the technical tasks assigned to the former and the data strategies assigned to the latter.

- *Reskill and Upskill for Data Visualization and AutoML*: Organizations need to leverage their employees, especially for Data Visualization, as well as the increasingly important area of AutoML or AutoAI. The visualization market is quite mature with tools such as Tableau [29]. AutoML is more challenging but also more promising in terms of business value. Many software vendors are starting to provide robust solutions for AutoML. Therefore, following and re-skilling Citizen Data Scientists from Visualization to AutoML is critical.

- *Digital Design Sprints* (Chapter 6) – being lean and effective: Check the following [30] on the Sprint methodology [31], which takes about 4-5 days. There is a perfect fit either during or immediately post the 4–5-day to leverage Low Code/No Code Data Science platforms for a Minimum Viable Product (MVP).

- *Watch emerging platforms and tools:* The Citizen Data Science domain is relatively new. It is essential to watch and re-assess Citizen Data Scientist tooling as these emerge. For example, a relatively new C3 AI Machina [32] tool " simplifies access to data and enables drag-and-drop application of powerful machine learning and AI models." There are other tools, and new ones are constantly emerging.

Data Science is multi-faceted and complex. We are witnessing the emergence of tools that enable citizens to efficiently conduct data cleansing, visualization and even harvesting insights from data automatically: another key and formidable trend to alleviate Digital Transformation Debt.

References

[1]   https://www.rtinsights.com/can-the-enterprise-in-motion-be-autonomic/

[2]   https://web-assets.domo.com/blog/wp-content/uploads/2017/07/17_domo_data-never-sleeps-5-01.png

[3]   https://www.accenture.com/in-en/insight-explainable-citizen-ai

[4]   https://www.rtinsights.com/process-data-its-about-time/

[5]   https://www.amazon.com/Developing-Applications-Kaufmann-Management-Systems/dp/1558601473

[6]   https://www.amazon.com/Object-Oriented-Databases-Setrag-Khoshafian/dp/0471570583

[7]   https://www.techopedia.com/definition/8714/object-relational-database-ord

[8]   https://searchdatamanagement.techtarget.com/definition/NoSQL-Not-Only-SQL

[9]   https://whatis.techtarget.com/definition/3Vs

[10]   https://www.scribd.com/document/407801536/AWS-Data-Lake-eBook

[11]   https://aws.amazon.com/products/storage/data-lake-storage/

[12]   http://en.wikipedia.org/wiki/Database_administrator

[13]   https://hostingdata.co.uk/nosql-database/

[14]   http://www.forbes.com/sites/oreillymedia/2012/01/19/volume-velocity-variety-what-you-need-to-know-about-big-data/

[15]   http://en.wikipedia.org/wiki/Internet_of_Things

[16]   https://www.mygreatlearning.com/blog/what-is-data-science/#whatisdatascience

[17]   https://www.superdatascience.com/

[18]   https://www.cheetahdigital.com/blog/liberating-your-customer-data-citizen-data-scientist

[19]   https://www.gartner.com/en/newsroom/press-releases/2017-01-16-gartner-says-more-than-40-percent-of-data-science-tasks-will-be-automated-by-2020

[20]   https://www.tableau.com/products/prep

[21]   https://parabola.io/

[22]   https://www.infoworld.com/article/3430788/automated-machine-learning-or-automl-explained.html

[23]   https://cloud.google.com/automl

[24]   https://www.ibm.com/cloud/watson-studio/autoai

[25]   https://www.datarobot.com/wiki/citizen-data-scientist/

[26]   https://www.datarobot.com/wiki/target/

[27]   https://www.datarobot.com/wiki/feature-engineering/

[28]   https://www.datarobot.com/wiki/training-validation-holdout/

[29]   https://www.tableau.com/

[30]   https://www.linkedin.com/pulse/going-lean-during-quarantine-dr-setrag-khoshafian/

[31]   https://www.amazon.com/Sprint-Solve-Problems-Test-Ideas/dp/150112174X/

[32]   https://c3.ai/live/no-code-ai-for-citizen-data-scientists/

Chapter 6: Design Thinking Innovation

The previous chapters - especially Chapter 2 to Chapter 5 - focused on technologies that enhance Operational Excellence and empower Citizen Developers and Citizen Data Scientists. Culture (Chapter 1) should lead enterprises to innovation - which is critical for alleviating Digital Transformation Debt. This Chapter focuses on pragmatic innovation approaches through the increasingly popular Design Thinking Methodology [1] leveraging digital technologies.

Design Thinking can be used both by startups for faster and more successful Minimum Viable Products or incumbent enterprises on their transformation journeys.

Design Thinking Methodology, as described here, incorporates the Design Sprint [2] followed by Minimum Viable Product (MVP) development using Low Code/No Code platforms.

The post-COVID-19 Mandate for Innovation

The COVID-19 pandemic was a Black Swan [3] event par excellence—even though some dispute [4] this characterization. The author of Black Swan—Nassim Nicholas Taleb—has another equally compelling perspective in Antifragile—Things That Gain from Disorder [5]. Here is what he says on anti-fragility that is so relevant to this discussion:

> *Entrepreneurship is a risky and heroic activity, necessary for growth or even the mere survival of the economy.*

Spot on. Entrepreneurship should be the mantra of all organizations: incumbents, large and small, or startups. Entrepreneurial innovation accentuates the acceleration of experimenting, deploying, and abandoning legacy organizational structures in favor of bold, innovative alternative cultures and solutions at all organizational levels.

> *Innovation culture needs to become the prevailing epitome for all organizations.*

Even back in 2019, an MIT Sloan & Deloitte article [6] drove home the cultural challenges: "The history of technological advance in business is littered with examples of companies focusing on technologies without investing in organizational capabilities that ensure their impact. In many companies, (failures are) classic examples of expectations falling short because organizations didn't change mindsets and processes or build cultures that fostered change."

We witnessed many innovative organizations in healthcare [7], manufacturers [8], pharmaceutical companies [9], and restaurants [10] re-define and re-organize their priorities for COVID-19 products and services at an unprecedented rate. We are also witnessed innovative startups re-aligning their services [11], given the constraints of COVID-19.

Now more than ever, enterprises need to be in-motion [12]—that is, embarking upon anti-fragile transformation, with digital technologies helping them continuously innovate for tangible results. Enterprises that embark upon the "motion" journey will face some resistance, especially in the get-go.

Digital technologies are moving at a highly rapid pace. Indeed, the movement to the Cloud, Robotics [13], the Rise of Connected Things (IoT) [14], and perhaps the most disruptive of them all: Blockchain [15] – are just some of the technologies that will shape (and potentially make or break) companies in the next few years.

The culture challenge here, is that of speed in assimilating these technologies while at the same time prioritizing a culture of innovation for the discovery and fast development of viable products or services. After all, we have heard of "fail fast but succeed faster." Technologies such as Blockchain [16] (which is the foundation of cryptocurrencies [17] - (Chapter 9)) have profound pragmatic implications [18] that will empower a new generation of innovators and potentially disrupt all industries.

Innovation is not about digital technologies for technologies' sake. The preceding Chapters on Citizen Developers (Chapter 4) and Citizen Data Scientists (Chapter 5) are critical. Process and Data [19] are complimentary. Organizations will realize they need to shift the Culture from the old system of bulk marketing, siloed organizations, and ad-hoc experiences to a digitally transformed 1:1 connected customer engagement. Connected Devices [20] (IoT - Chapter 8) will increasingly become customer engagement channels [21] (Chapter 7).

Design Thinking

"Design is not just what it looks like and feels like. Design is how it works." - Steve Jobs

Design Thinking is a relatively new approach for organizations that helps them to innovate through empathizing with their target customers, ideating, and promptly developing innovative solutions [22]. This is often followed by testing and deployment. The entire Design Thinking process is a dynamic one, with multiple continuous iterations between the phases.

Design Thinking engages multiple disciplines' efforts and creates a prioritized backlog of innovative solutions – balancing ease of development, optimized customer experiences, market opportunities, and business value. Design Thinking engages various innovators to think big, think innovation, think digital – but start small [23]. It also involves design methods and processes [24].

The success of entrepreneurs and founders in startups is often contingent upon factors beyond that of innovation, marketing, and a sales strategy –for example, methodologies from Ideation to Minimum Viable Products (MVP) and then productization. Design Thinking is one such methodology that could help balance innovation with achievable execution for success.

The overall approach involves Design Thinking Methodology, Design Sprint, and Low Code/No Code platforms for Minimum Viable Products (MVP) in a post-COVID-19 era.

The following illustrates the Design Thinking Methodology:

- The *Definition* phase scopes the market opportunity with a clear statement that is both actionable and measurable and achievable. This phase defines a clear focus of what the innovation entails.

- The *Research* phase uses techniques such as Personas, Interviews, and Observations to discover the needs and prioritize *Customers*, which is especially relevant to the innovation's essential focus.

- The *Interpretation* phase uses empathy techniques to consider the emotions of the Customers. It also uses techniques such as the Fishbone Diagram to map the cause and effect.

- The *Ideation* phase involves brainstorming [25] techniques and collaborative sessions to think up innovative ideas. Prioritization in this phase balances business value with ease of implementation to identify the low hanging fruits.

- The *Prototype* phase, much like the name suggests, turns the low hanging fruit into demonstrable solution forms. These forms can be used to get immediate and early feedback from the target personas.

- The *Evaluation* phase, tests and refines the prototype(s) through persona feedback and iterations.

Prioritization

Prioritization is an essential milestone in *Ideation*. A robust Prioritization workshop or effort progresses through the following phases:

- *Specific criteria for Prioritization*: this is the criteria ideation phase for Prioritization. The goal is to balance ease of implementation with business value and market penetration.

- *Individual Contributor Ideation*: Each workshop member comes up with several innovative ideas – resulting in guided "Brain Dump" with the criteria driving their recommendations. The workgroup members must work independently in this phase, and without external pressures.

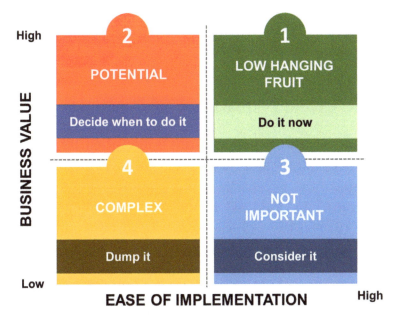

- *Consolidated Group Ideation*: If there are enough participants, the workshop members are broken into groups for group discussions. Ideally, each group will have representation from the different personas. During this phase, the individual ideas are first discussed to see if there are affinities or similarities between the individual recommendations from the previous ideation phase. Typically, there will be clusters with several outliers. Next, the group will discuss and place the recommendations in four Prioritization groups:

1. *Pursue – High Priority*: Low Hanging Fruit
2. *Potential (aka Luxury) – Medium Priority*: Decide when to do it.

3. *Support – Medium Priority*: Not that important, but consider it.
4. *Avoid – Low Priority*: Dump it

Prototype and Evaluation

Once the target low-hanging fruit is identified, it requires further refining – and then needs to be prototyped and evaluated for potential improvement. Subsequently, it needs to be followed with actual Minimum Viable Products (MVPs). However, before embarking and developing the MVP leveraging Low Code/No Code platforms, the recommended approach for Prototyping and Evaluation is the related methodology called Design Sprint [26], whose practice is captured in the book with the same name – by Jake Knapp.

Here is the essence of Design Sprint [27] – for Prototyping and Evaluation (aka Validation):

> *"The big idea with the Design Sprint is to build and test a prototype in just five days. You'll take a small team, clear the schedule for a week, and rapidly progress from problem to tested solution using a proven step-by-step checklist. It's like fast-forwarding into the future, so you can see how customers react before you investall the time and expense of building a real product."*

The five days of the Design Sprint [28] culminate with Prototyping and Evaluation (aka Validate).

5-days, with all the critical stakeholders, sounds like a lot of effort. It is a serious commitment. However, despite its seemingly cumbersome nature—it is crucial for success. At its core, it is a *lean enterprise* approach—with the operative word being "lean." Many startups fail because they lack a rigorous yet robust methodology to come up with and evaluate a given prototype.

Virtual collaboration is particularly relevant. Some tools can significantly assist the collaboration of Design Thinking. For instance, Miro [29] is a powerful and robust visual collaboration and whiteboarding platform that includes the Design Sprint template. Other tools such as InVision [30] can be used to conduct a mockup of the prototype and subsequently validate or evaluate it with the real users.

Chapter 4 elaborated on the Citizen Developer leveraging Low Code/No Code platforms regarding rapid prototyping and Validation. As noted, there are a plethora of tools with different styles and options:

- Web & Mobile Application Low Code/No Code Platforms

- Business Process Management Low Code/No Code Platforms

- Database Management Low Code/No Code Platforms

- Automated Integration Low Code/No Code Platforms

- Niche Low Code/No Code Platforms: e-commerce, blockchain, AI, CRM, ERP, etc.

Increasingly, instead of "throw-away" mockups – innovative organizations can instead jump earlier and leverage one or more Low Code/No Code platforms for the purpose of prototyping and evaluation. The alternative is to follow up with the refinements that invariably result from Day 5 of the Design Sprint methodology. In other words, Design Sprint is followed up with a Low Code/ No Code development of the Minimum Viable Product that reflects the "low hanging fruit." It is a *Do it Now* prerogative, with an actual deployed implementation.

Recommendations

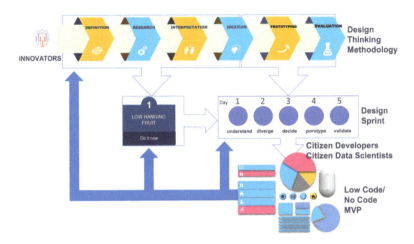

In the post-COVID-19 era, innovation with anti-fragile agility is no longer an option. However, as highlighted above, startups and incumbent enterprises need to adopt three essential best practices:

- *Design Thinking*: This is the overarching methodology that should be platform or technology-agnostic, where organizations can select, implement, and deploy the MVP that corresponds to the low-hanging fruit prioritization. Do it now!

- *Design Sprint*: This 5-day Design Sprint approach at the tail of Design Thinking Methodology aligns and realizes the Prototyping and Evaluation phases, especially Prototyping and Validation in a Design sprint. The 5-day sprint conclusion is, at the very least, a mocked-up version of the Low Hanging Fruit that is the MVP's predecessor.

- *Low Code/No Code Platform Selection*: There are now hundreds of Low Code/No Code platforms with a range of capabilities and pricing. Selection is not easy, but it is undoubtedly critical for success. The startup or enterprise needs to approach the selection objectively, identifying the platform that fits best its needs for the MVP.

- *MVP Implementation and Deployment*: This is the ultimate objective of Design Thinking – and the beginning of the iterations for continuous improvement and market penetration.

References

[1]   https://www.amazon.com/Design-Thinking-Methodology-Emrah-Yayici-ebook/dp/B01N47J13I/

[2]   https://www.thesprintbook.com/how

[3]   https://www.amazon.com/Black-Swan-Improbable-Robustness-Fragility/dp/081297381X

[4]   https://www.newyorker.com/news/daily-comment/the-pandemic-isnt-a-black-swan-but-a-portent-of-a-more-fragile-global-system

[5]   https://www.amazon.com/Ant%20fragile-Things-Disorder-ANTIFRAGILE-Paperback/dp/B00QORW08I/

[6]   https://sloanreview.mit.edu/projects/strategy-drives-digital-transformation/

[7]   https://www.hcinnovationgroup.com/covid-19

[8]   https://www.theverge.com/2020/4/15/21222219/general-motors-ventec-ventilators-ford-tesla-coronavirus-covid-19

[9]   https://www.pharmaceutical-technology.com/comment/covid-19-pharmaceutical-companies-impact/

[10]   https://www.bonappetit.com/story/food-businesses-covid-19

[11]   https://www.glendaleca.gov/government/departments/economic-development/emergency-business-resources/creative-business-solutions

[12]   https://www.rtinsights.com/what-is-the-enterprise-in-motion/

[13]   https://www.academia.edu/37259120/The_Adaptive_Digital_Factory

[14]   https://www.linkedin.com/pulse/2017-iot-digital-transformation-internet-setrag-khoshafian/

[15]   https://en.wikipedia.org/wiki/Blockchain

[16]   https://www.linkedin.com/pulse/blockchain-valuechain-setrag-khoshafian/

[17]   https://blockgeeks.com/guides/what-is-cryptocurrency/

[18]   http://contact.samsungsds.com/blockchain-warranty-management

[19]   https://www.rtinsights.com/process-data-its-about-time/

[20]   https://www.linkedin.com/pulse/transforming-customer-relationship-culture-setrag-khoshafian/

[21]   https://cognitiveworld.com/articles/ai-driving-digital-customer-engagement-part-i

[22]   https://www.amazon.com/Best-Practices-Knowledge-Workers-Special-ebook/dp/B01FTC8IEI/pfingara

[23]   https://www.forbes.com/sites/cognitiveworld/2018/09/14/digital-transformation-debt-part-ii/?sh=772559f0112d

[24]   https://en.wikipedia.org/wiki/Design_thinking

[25]   https://www.youtube.com/watch?v=ksyiaymXcN4&feature=youtu.be

[26]   https://www.thesprintbook.com/buy

[27]   https://uxknowledgebase.com/design-sprint-f53b126b1e02

[28]   http://critical.digital/discussing-design-sprints-with-kevin-rose-jake-knapp-and-daniel-burka/847

[29]   https://miro.com/

[30]   https://www.invisionapp.com/

Chapter 7: Customer Experience Optimization

This Chapter builds upon the previous chapters - especially on innovation (Chapter 6) to focus on the most impactful and relevant trend of Digital Transformation: *the customer*. The customer in the digital era is always connected, tech-savvy, and has high expectations. Customer Experience (CX) Optimization is, therefore, a critical dimension that cannot be overlooked, particularly

in the new era ushered in by the COVID-19 pandemic. CX can be realized through leveraging AI [1] (Chapter 5), innovative design (Chapter 6), and Automation [2] (Chapter 3). DX transformation elucidates the need to shift from bulk marketing, siloed organizations, and ad-hoc experiences to digitally transformed 1:1 connected customer engagements. The combination of AI with digitized end-to-end value streams on behalf of the customer creates this experience through extreme Personalization [3] that leads to concrete business results, such as improvements in Net Promoter Scores (NPS) [4].

The post-COVID-19 Mandate for CX

There has been multiple COVID-19 customer experience [5] impact studies. One of these studies in particular [6] showed that 72% of consumers preferred to connect via digital channels. There was also a significant increase in choosing digital self-service options—this was especially true among the millennial and GenZ generations. On the flip side, customer satisfaction and the overall customer experience quality are of paramount importance now. 73% of customers indicated they would sever ties with organizations that gave them even one poor experience.

KPMG has been conducting studies on customer experience and has gathered six universal sets of qualities that have impacted customer experience, year after year. The following are the six pillars [7] from KPMG:

The new reality of customer experience [8] has prioritized Personalization and Integrity. As companies demonstrate their commitment to a safe and secure environment and seek to adapt to customers' unique circumstances – the factors of Integrity and Personalization now play a particularly vital role in driving both advocacy and loyalty.

- Integrity is the most vital driver of Advocacy (NPS) across 18 of the 27 markets, while Personalization leads across 8 markets.
- Personalization is the strongest pillar in driving Customer Loyalty in 19 of the 27 markets, while Integrity leads across 6 markets.

Not surprisingly, being an autonomic enterprise in motion with effective responsiveness, agility, and anti-fragility allows organizations to better cope with the coming challenges.

Optimizing the Customer Experience: The NPS

You may have been asked in a short survey after using a product or a service: on a scale of 1-10, would you recommend the product/service to someone else (e.g., a friend, a relative, or a colleague)?

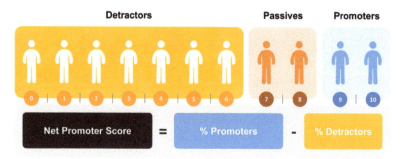

The NPS is calculated based on the answer to this simple survey question. Introduced by Frederick F. Reichheld [9] in 2003, this is fundamentally a survey about a customer's willingness to recommend a product or company to their network of friends and acquaintances. Promoters are those who scale 9-10. The score is the difference between promoters and detractors (0-6). What should the scores be? As indicated here [10], "50 and above is excellent, and 70 and above is the best of the best." Here are some of the leaders by industry [11]:

Industry	Leader	Leader's NPS
Airlines	Southwest	71
Auto Insurance	USAA	73
Banking	USAA	69
Brokerage / Investments	Vanguard	67
Cable / Satellite TV	Verizon Fios	24
Cellular Phone Service	Cricket Wireless	54
Credit Cards	USAA	73
Department / Specialty Stores	Costco	76
Drug Stores / Pharmacies	Walmart Pharmacy	34
Grocery / Supermarkets	H-E-B	65
Health Insurance	Kaiser Permanente	34
Home / Contents Insurance	USAA	72
Hotels	Ritz Carlton	70
Internet Service	AT&T Fiber	20
Laptop Computers	Apple	62
Life Insurance	USAA	63
Online Entertainment	Apple Music	55
Online Shopping	samsclub.com	60
Shipping Services	DHL	38
Smartphones	Apple	51

The post-COVID-19 Customer Experience Shifts

Significant era shifts are happening in customer experience optimization. The new generation of customers is quite tech-savvy as they leverage social media extensively and have come to expect instant change because of this. They also want to be treated differently or uniquely—based on their history, background, or situation. As noted above, Integrity and Personalization are the top requirements where this is concerned. The following illustrates the shifts from traditional to post-COVID-19. They also highlight the DX technologies that are leveraged for each shift.

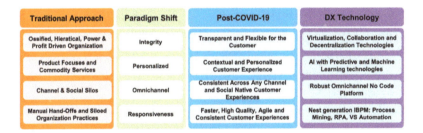

Traditional Approach	Paradigm Shift	Post-COVID-19	DX Technology
Ossified, Hieratical, Power & Profit Driven Organization	Integrity	Transparent and Flexible for the Customer	Virtualization, Collaboration and Decentralization Technologies
Product Focuses and Commodity Services	Personalized	Contextual and Personalized Customer Experience	AI with Predictive and Machine Learning technologies
Channel & Social Silos	Omnichannel	Consistent Across Any Channel and Social Native Customer Experiences	Robust Omnichannel No Code Platform
Manual Hand-Offs and Siloed Organization Practices	Responsiveness	Faster, High Quality, Agile and Consistent Customer Experiences	Nest generation IBPM: Process Mining, RPA, VS Automation

There is no doubt about it. In the COVID-19 era—Digital Technology has become an indispensable tool for driving customer engagement. For many companies, effective digital solutions build B2C, B2B, and B2B2C relationships. Technology fills gaps where legacy or manual systems could not – allowing businesses to create personalized, intelligent, and user-friendly journeys for a wide range of consumers.

Integrity

The crux of "integrity" is trust between the enterprise and the customer. Integrity encompasses honesty, delivery on promises, high moral principles, and ethical behavior. The old norm of being primarily profit-focused is giving way to more environmentally and socially responsible actions.

While customers often do not have visibility to the company's culture, enterprises' behavior and Integrity manifest their internal organizational structure. We covered cultural transformation in the first Chapter. Virtual meetings and virtual presence have had both an equalizing and flattening effect on most organizations. The COVID-19 pandemic, then, provides a robust opportunity for organizations to re-assess the rigidity of their current structures and flatten their organizations.

Technologies: Integrity is primarily moral and cultural, but several digital technologies could assist in the post-COVID-19 era. These include Virtualization [12], digitization of policies and value streams [13], as well as Automation [14]. In inter-enterprise interaction, decentralization technologies such as Blockchain [15] can play a pivotal role. This will be covered in Chapter 9.

Personalized

The new generation of customers, particularly Millennials, are increasingly tech-savvy and digitally

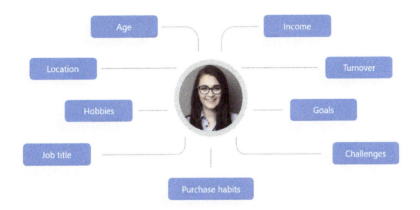

chatty. And in the COVID-19 era, they have become even chattier! With their mobile and connected devices, they are active and continuously engaged through social interactions on various social platforms. Above all, they are demanding experiences that are a unique blend of contextual, meaningful, instantaneous, and entertaining. Additionally, social networking channels have given them a powerful voice—the voice of the network [16]—allowing them to instantly provide feedback (both good and bad) and share ideas about products, services, and companies.

Different customers would like to be treated differently: through useful, meaningful interactions, offers, or decisions on their behalf that are specifically relevant to their context—the crux of Personalization can be achieved.

Technologies: Artificial Intelligence with Predictive and Machine Learning [17] algorithms is a critical enabler for Personalization. Increasingly Citizen Data Scientists [18] (Chapter 5) can achieve Personalization objectives—primarily through next-generation Customer Relationship Management (CRM) platforms [19].

Omnichannel

Omni means "all-encompassing." In the context of Customer Experience Optimization, it means consistently supporting different channels and all modes of interactions between a service or solution provider and the customer. This means the customer can interact via a browser, mobile device, service representative, IVR (interactive voice response), or other channels. This "consistency" also means that the customer's experience involving the solution's capabilities is identical.

Omni also means he/she can start an interaction through one channel and then seamlessly switch to continue through another while maintaining the interaction's context and integrity. For example, in an insurance application, an insured or claimant interaction can commence in one channel (say a tablet) and move to another channel (e.g., a browser) while maintaining full context for the customer.

Technologies: Next-generation CRM and Low Code/No Code platforms [20] (Chapter 4) support Omnichannel responsive and native applications. Here also, Citizen Developers [21] are getting involved to optimize the customer experience from a business perspective.

Responsiveness

Real-time or near real-time responsiveness is critical for Customer Experience Optimizations. Responsiveness encompasses both the time and the quality of the customer experience. It also means the organization needs to know when and how quickly to involve a human response vs. automated bots or virtual assistants. Responsiveness will be challenging to achieve without the transformations of archaic cultures. This temporal dimension often involves service levels for a timely response to customer service requests that are on target. It also applies to product or service transactions—with timely responses to inquiries or sales cycles. But time is only one dimension. The other—often ignored—is quality.

There is very much a Real-Time Lean Six Sigma [22] (Chapter 2 and Chapter 3) principle here. Lean focuses on reducing waste and improving Customer Experience processes. Six Sigma, on the other hand, attempts to improve quality while reducing variation. Real-Time means the optimizations for Responsiveness involving efficiency, timeliness, and high quality is achieved in real-time (vs. retroactively after analyzing the data). This is of paramount importance for customer experience optimization.

Technologies: Organizations are structured vertically. However, Responsiveness to business value generation typically involves multiple business units or participants— in other words—*through horizontal organizational* *integration.* Organizations in the post-COVID-19 landscape need to be responsive through digitizing and automating their value streams. Automation involving bots, virtual assistants, and Automation of processes are the critical enablers for responsiveness.

Recommendations

Optimizing the Customer Experience is paramount for all organizations. We have seen some of these recommendations in previous Chapters. It is essential to consider them in the CX context too.

- *Cultural Shift for Integrity*: The first recommendation is to embark upon a Servant Leadership (Chapter 1) journey and flatten the organization. In other words, changing the Culture toward a truly customer-centric model. This also means empowering all the levels of the organization and treating your different employees differently. Contextual management and empowerment should be strategic priorities; they are essential for Integrity.

- *Selection of Platforms—balancing capability with cost*: Selecting the right combination of platforms becomes more complex for Customer Experience Optimization. First, there is the selection of the CRM platform. Second, there is the empowerment of Citizen Developers (Chapter 4) and Citizen Data Scientists (Chapter 5). Third, there are Automation tools—

from virtual assistants, bots, No Code platforms, and automation tools.

- *Strategize to treat different customers differently*: Personalization should be a prioritized strategy post-COVID-19. It should not be reduced to a marketing gimmick. Personalization is not easy, and it requires both the right corporate mindset and technologies—but it is imperative. The new generation of customers is demanding to be treated differently. Digitally Transformed organizations need to continuously innovate (Chapter 6) to meet this requirement.

- *Continuously Measure and Improve*: Select a measurement methodology and constantly analyze the feedback. Net Promoter score is one approach and has proven to be quite useful, but it is not the only one. Optimizing Customer Experience is complex. The technologies to drill down from measures to cause-effect and root-cause analysis are critical.

- *Empower your Citizens*: For Integrity, Personalization, Omnichannel solutions, and Responsiveness, you need Citizens: Citizen Developers and Citizen Data Scientists. As noted in Chapter 6, the Design Thinking with Design Sprints and MVPs should be part of the organization's DNA embarking upon the CX Optimization journey. Through identifying and empowering your Citizens—you will be amazed by what they can achieve with some encouragement.

References

[1]   https://cognitiveworld.com/articles/ai-driving-digital-customer-engagement-part-i

[2]   https://cognitiveworld.com/articles/ai-driving-digital-customer-engagement-part-ii

[3]   https://conversionsciences.com/personalization-examples/

[4]   https://en.wikipedia.org/wiki/Net_Promoter

[5]   https://www.mckinsey.com/business-functions/operations/our-insights/elevating-customer-experience-excellence-in-the-next-normal

[6]   https://devsitel.wpengine.com/covid-19-customer-experience-impact-study/

[7]   https://assets.kpmg/content/dam/kpmg/be/pdf/2017/customer-experience-the-next-battleground-for-success.pdf

[8]   https://assets.kpmg/content/dam/kpmg/xx/pdf/2020/07/customer-experience-in-the-new-reality.pdf

[9]   https://en.wikipedia.org/wiki/Fred_Reichheld

[10]   https://blog.hubspot.com/service/what-is-a-good-net-promoter-score

[11]   https://www.satmetrix.com/wp-content/uploads/2020/07/net-promoter-score-benchmarks.pdf

[12]   https://www.rtinsights.com/covid-19-it-challenges/

[13]   https://cognitiveworld.com/articles/2020/8/1/2-operational-excellence-amp-vsaas-digital-transformation-debts-post-covid-19

[14]   https://cognitiveworld.com/articles/2020/8/23/3-automation-digital-transformation-debts-post-covid-19

[15]   https://cognitiveworld.com/articles/blockchain-valuechain

[16]   https://www.linkedin.com/pulse/transforming-customer-relationship-culture-setrag-khoshafian/

[17]   https://www.scribd.com/document/237925426/Adaptive-BPM-for-Adaptive-Enterprises-WP-May2012-FINAL

[18]   https://cognitiveworld.com/articles/2020/10/19/5-citizen-data-scientist-digital-transformation-debts-post-covid-19

[19]   https://www.scribd.com/document/197759358/Intelligent-BPM-the-Next-Wave-for-Customer-Centric-Business-Applications-Khoshafian

[20]   https://www.startupassistant.io/blog/no-codelow-code-mvps

[21]   https://cognitiveworld.com/articles/2020/9/27/4-no-code-citizen-developers-digital-transformation-debts-post-covid-19

[22]   https://www.rtinsights.com/four-intelligent-automation-methodologies-one-objective/

Chapter 8: IoT Connectivity

This and the next Chapter will focus on the Connected and Decentralized World. They build upon the previous Chapters and are two key Digital Transformation pillars.

We are rapidly moving to a fully connected world—with billions of devices in our homes, cities, and workplaces that are all on the Internet. Connectivity through the Internet of Things (IoT) is becoming ubiquitous [1].

Here we focus on alleviating Digital Transformation Debt through Internet of Things (IoT). Though a bit slow in comprehensive market penetration, both the Consumer Internet of Things [2] as well as the Industrial Internet of Things [3] (IIoT) are beginning to transform homes, businesses, and governments as well as heavy industries such as discrete and process Manufacturing. This transformation is accelerating in the post-COVID-19 era.

IoT has many applications addressing challenges emanating from the disruptions in Supply Chain, Manufacturing, Public Sector services, and, most importantly, Healthcare. IoT connected devices are exploding. The road to IoT success, though, runs through Digital Process Automation [4] (Chapter 3)—which we have now identified as Intelligent Process Automation of Things [5]—connecting the consumer's world through end-to-end value streams that orchestrate people, things, enterprise applications, and business partners.

Intelligent Process Automation of Things (IPAoT)

Many components and technologies are employed to support IoT/IIoT use cases end-to-end: from the Edges to the Enterprise - involving People, Processes, Analytics (from Thing Data), and of course, Connected Devices. There are also IoT reference models that pertain to IoT consortia and standardization bodies. My favorite is always the IoT World Forum's Reference Model [6]. This 7-level architecture reference model prioritizes

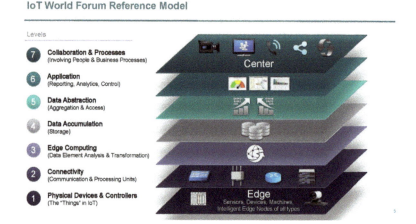

IoT World Forum Reference Model

collaboration and Business Processes at the top of the multi-level architecture for IoT.

Intelligence of Things: Insight to Action

IoT generates an enormous amount of data. We are inundated with information from connected devices—both in consumer and industrial contexts, and this does not appear to be showing signs of easing off any time soon. Connected devices are becoming increasingly significant sources of information: Big Data is becoming "Thing Data" [7]. Over time, this *Thing Data* will be stored, analyzed, and mined for models that reflect *insights* – that can then be acted upon—such as an analytics model that can predict that a device will fail before it happens.

The following illustrates the continuous improvement loop, from Insight to Action. At the bottom, you have the raw data emanating from connected IoT/IIoT devices. The

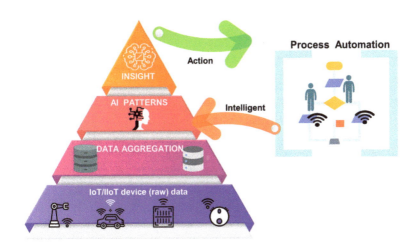

raw data could also include customer transaction data, trading partner data, and even Blockchain transactions.

With Intelligent Process Automation of Things (IPAoT), connected devices (IoT), people, enterprise applications (ERPs), and trading partners can collaborate and achieve objectives end-to-end. Equally important is the Intelligence that drives the processes in each step and each state toward the objective. The AI patterns discovered from the Thing Data are operationalized and acted upon within the context of automated processes. Thus, AI is leveraged for optimizing the operation of the devices in real-time—where it assists people intelligently, automating the work wherever it makes sense.

Edge Computing

IoT connected devices are at the edges, which is the lowest level of the Enterprise-In-Motion ecosystem.

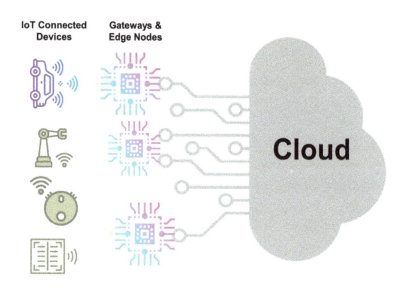

The Internet of Things (IoT) and the Industrial Internet of Things (IIoT) are significant contributors to Digital Transformation.

When it comes to autonomic IoT, the emerging connected devices trend is Edge Computing [8]. What is becoming increasingly clear, is that business logic and AI models can run at the IoT edges. There are many advantages to executing AI models at the edge [9]. In many applications, instantaneous decisions need to be made to deal with, for instance, hazardous material or dangerous levels of pollution, or perhaps even emergency dispatching. The delays of roundtripping from a Cloud-based data center for AI model execution could be prohibitive.

In some cases, Internet connectivity might engender unacceptable latencies or even be offline. The actuators and sensors of connected devices often leverage gateways to connect to the Cloud. These connected devices as well as the gateways are becoming increasingly powerful in storage, computation, and networking optimizations. Pushing computations and intelligence to the edges reduces the latency of executions.

The Industrial Internet Consortium [10] defines it as follows: "Edge computing is a decentralized computing infrastructure in which computing resources and application services can be distributed along the communication path from the data source to the cloud." Edge computing allows devices to take immediate action. In other words, edge computing is faster and more optimized.

Digital Prescriptive Maintenance: The Killer IoT Application

Digital Prescriptive Maintenance [11] leverages IPAoT, taking it beyond predictive analytics and prescribing precisely what needs to be done, by whom and when— leveraging end-to-end digitized value streams or processes. IPAoT determines the remaining useful life [12] of a device and takes predictive and proactive action before it breaks. This is why we called it *digital*

prescriptive maintenance; it implies the Digitization and Automation of the prescribed tasks to resolve the maintenance case. Above is an example of end-to-end prescriptive maintenance—from detection and creation of the case, to triaging, field service dispatching, supplier provisioning, and warranty.

IoT post-COVID-19

The pandemic exposed the vulnerability of both the private and public sectors in managing their respective assets. There were products, such as hand sanitizers or Webcams, that were either difficult to source or expensive where available. With IoT, the assets can be the manufactured goods, or the assets can be the connected devices themselves. They could be simple devices with low energy and communication bandwidth capabilities that need a more sophisticated gateway to connect to the Cloud. In the Industrial Internet context, powerful connected devices have onboard computing capabilities that allow them to process data at the edges and connect to the Cloud through Wi-Fi or 5G connections.

Alternatively, RFID could be attached and embedded in the packaging of the goods for manufactured goods – for instance, in transportation with containers.

- *Telehealth and COVID-19*: There has been a recent spike in Telehealth [13]. IoT, with connected medical devices [14], plays a significant role: "The Internet of Things (IoT) has extended traditional videoconference visits to enable practitioners to remotely monitor patients' [15] blood pressure, oxygenation levels, pulse and other key metrics." More importantly, it is not just about sensing. Telehealth needs digitized and automated processes. As indicated by one of the experts Dr. Peter Fleischut [16]: "It's about people, process and technology ... It's probably 80% people, 15% process and 5% technology." Once again, Culture (i.e., People) is more important than technology (Chapter 1).

- *Industry 4.0*: Even before the pandemic, manufacturers were introducing Automation, sophisticated robotics, and edge computing in all phases of the supply chain. With COVID-19 still looming on the horizon, Robotics and Automation are becoming critical in Industry 4.0. The manufacturing industry—especially automotive original equipment manufacturers (OEMs)—were in a significant digital transition, and COVID-19 served as a catalyst to accelerate this transformation. Service levels of assets—often parts in supply chain applications—could be critical. Automation is also increasingly deployed at the edges, which alleviates or reduces the need for human interventions or contact.

The opportunities for addressing COVID-19 challenges pertain to tracking people's movements, provisioning, and the delivery of supplies:

- *Tracking People*: Many countries are leveraging IoT technologies to track people. For example, South Korea's Ministry of Interior and Safety has developed an app that uses GPS to track [17] those ordered to quarantine. Not all tracking is good, and it could even be dangerous - violating privacy. IoT is just the technology. Ethical policies should control IoT tracking.

- *Supply Chain Tracking and Optimizations*: IoT tracking is becoming increasingly important in the end-to-end supply chains [18], primarily due to the pandemic disruptions [19]. End-to-end asset visibility is becoming a requirement for manufacturers— including optimization of service level agreements for end-to-end delivery of the connected assets.

- *IoT Intelligence at the Edges*: COVID-19 responses need to be real-time and intelligent. In many applications, the delays of roundtripping from a Cloud-based data center for AI model execution could be prohibitive. Increasingly business logic and AI models are executing at the IoT edges [20]. There are many advantages to executing AI models at the edge.

Let us look at a couple of Healthcare service Internet of Medical Things (IoMT)[21] examples.

Whoop   Kinsa

- Kinsa [22]: Fever is considered one of the leading indicators of COVID-19 infection. Kinsa has millions of connected thermometer consumers and is collaborating with local governments and health authorities—as temperature screening remains critical for inhibiting the spread of COVID-19. The temperature data of the connected thermometer is aggregated anonymously and displayed per county.

- Whoop [23] is a fitness tracker with a band and mobile app that can monitor various health measures such as heart rate variability, resting heart rate, and sleep. Whoop responded to the current pandemic by updating their mobile app to monitor and interpret respiratory rates—since COVID-19 attacks the lungs. Therefore, monitoring respiration is critical [24] in managing COVID-19. Monitoring respiration "helps determine how much change you need to confidently conclude that a change is meaningful and not random variation. Median respiratory rate has a remarkably high signal to noise ratio, making it very easy to interpret and trust."

- GE Healthcare's Mural Virtual Care Solution [25] aggregates data and monitoring from several systems "into a single pane of glass providing hospitals the ability to extend clinical capabilities and resources by giving visibility to at-risk and ventilated patients while minimizing exposure to staff." This allows virtual monitoring through "near real-time data from ventilators, patient monitoring systems, electronic

medical records, labs, and other systems." The solution "allows one clinician to monitor several patients at once [26], supplementing existing monitoring devices in patients' rooms."

Recommendations

The post-COVID-19 era is a connected and truly globalized world! All industries are accelerating their Digital Transformation initiatives and IoT is a critical technology for DX. Here are our recommendations for alleviating IoT Digital Transformation Debt:

- *IoT Platforms and Interoperability*: IoT is complicated. There are more than 600 IoT platforms [27] for a plethora of IoT capabilities. Selecting the best-fit platform and solutions will be critical for success.

- *IoT No Code Development*: The emergence of Low Code/No Code Citizen Developers [28] (Chapter 4) for IoT will become critical. The enterprise needs to adopt competencies and best practices (Chapter 10) for IoT No Code Development—identifying the right tool for your needs.

- *Intelligent Process Automation of Things* (IPAoT) [5]: Any IoT strategy needs to include an end-to-end business process orchestration strategy. The road to IoT success runs through end-to-end value stream (Chapter 2) intelligent business process Automation

(Chapter 3). IPAoT needs an iBPM strategy. No Code/ Low Code process-centric IoT platforms are starting to emerge.

But perhaps most importantly, the focus of IoT initiatives should be on concrete ROI:

- *Subject Monitoring and Responding*: Monitoring to optimize insurance of Smart Homes [29], wellness tracking, health monitoring [30], Smart City transportation [31], connected car [32] applications in numerous Car-to-X (Car, Infrastructure, OEM)—to name a few.

- *Asset Monitoring and Responding*: There are compelling ROI while monitoring the connected asset's status or condition and then act—through IPAoT.

- *Data Monetization*: There are ROI opportunities through data monetization. Many Insurance companies [33]—especially automotive—leverage data to adjust Insurance costs depending on how you drive, etc.

- *Digital Prescriptive Maintenance*: This is the killer application for IoT. With AI analytics, it is possible to determine a device's remaining useful life [34] and take pro-active predictive action before it breaks.

References

[1]   https://www.eseye.com/resources/10-iot-trends-predictions-2021-
and-beyond/

[2]   https://www.cbronline.com/what-is/what-is-consumer-internet-of-
things-4926794/

[3]   https://www.academia.edu/37259120/The_Adaptive_Digital_Factory

[4]   https://www.linkedin.com/pulse/road-iot-success-runs-through-
dpa-setrag-khoshafian/

[5]   https://cognitiveworld.com/articles/2020/6/26/intelligent-process-
automation-of-things-ipaot

[6]   http://cdn.iotwf.com/resources/72/IoT_Reference_Model_04_
June_2014.pdf

[7]   https://www.informationweek.com/mobile/mobile-devices/rise-of-
things-iots-role-in-business-processes/a/d-id/1317010

[8]   https://blogs.cisco.com/tag/edge-computing

[9]   https://www.forbes.com/sites/forbestechcouncil/2020/04/06/
powering-the-edge-with-ai-in-an-iot-world/

[10]   https://www.iiconsortium.org/pdf/IIC_Edge_Computing_
Advantages_White_Paper_2019-10-24.pdf

[11]   https://theiotmagazine.com/the-iot-iiot-killer-application-digital-
prescriptive-maintenance-fddaa6db8616

[12]   https://www.mathworks.com/company/newsletters/articles/
three-ways-to-estimate-remaining-useful-life-for-predictive-
maintenance.html

[13]   https://www.iotworldtoday.com/2020/06/08/as-telehealth-spikes-
leading-organizations-shore-up-health-care-infrastructure/

[14]   https://theiotmagazine.com/digital-transformation-of-healthcare-
iomt-connectivity-ai-and-value-streams-62edc0f2be1a

[15]   https://www.iotworldtoday.com/2020/03/03/democratization-of-
patient-health-data-empowers-despite-data-quality-issues/

[16]   https://www.linkedin.com/in/pfleischut/

[17]   https://www.technologyreview.com/2020/03/06/905459/
        coronavirus-south-korea-smartphone-app-quarantine/

[18]   https://www.linkedin.com/pulse/digital-transformation-supply-
        chain-through-iot-setrag-khoshafian/

[19]   https://www.rfidjournal.com/rfid-and-iot-working-together-to-
        mitigate-covid-19-warehouse-disruptions

[20]   https://www.linkedin.com/pulse/intelligent-iot-edge-computing-dr-
        setrag-khoshafian/

[21]   https://healthtechmagazine.net/article/2020/01/how-internet-
        medical-things-impacting-healthcare-perfcon

[22]   https://www.kinsahealth.co/

[23]   https://www.whoop.com/thelocker/respiratory-rate-tracking-
        coronavirus/

[24]   https://www.shimmersensing.com/about/news/call-for-researchers-
        to-help-use-bioimpedance-to-manage-covid-19

[25]   https://www.gehealthcare.com/products/mural-virtual-care-
        solution

[26]   https://www.biospace.com/article/releases/ge-healthcare-deploys-
        remote-patient-data-monitoring-technology-to-help-clinicians-
        support-most-critical-covid-19-patients-across-the-health-system/

[27]   https://iot-analytics.com/iot-platform-companies-landscape-2020/

[28]   https://cognitiveworld.com/articles/2020/9/27/4-no-code-citizen-
        developers-digital-transformation-debts-post-covid-19

[29]   https://theiotmagazine.com/iot-digital-transformation-in-
        insurance-209cac56f496

[30]   https://aabme.asme.org/posts/internet-of-medical-things-
        revolutionizing-healthcare

[31]   https://www.masstlc.org/iot-digital-transformation-in-the-public-
        sector/

[32]   https://theiotmagazine.com/your-connected-vehicle-is-your-largest-wearable-523e7e99dc8e

[33]   https://www.bearingpoint.com/en-ch/our-success/insights/digital-transformation-in-the-insurance-industry-the-internet-of-things-as-a-main-driver/

[34]   https://medium.com/@RemiStudios/remaining-useful-life-in-predictive-maintenance-ffc91d7e4a97

Chapter 9: Blockchain Decentralization

Chapter 8 focused on the Connected World—through billions of IoT devices. This Chapter elaborates on the

complementary dimension of the Decentralized World - through Blockchain. Both are necessary for alleviating Digital Transformation Debt.

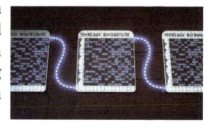

The price of Bitcoin (BTC) skyrocketed above $60,000 mid-March 2021 [1]. This is the highest it has ever been. Will it keep significantly increasing, or is this just a current hype or bubble? Who knows?

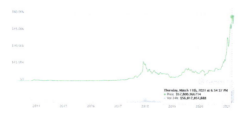

While cryptocurrencies undergo volatile changes, one thing remains certain: there have been many predictions of the demise of Bitcoin - being worthless and going down to zero. All of them have been false so far. *Blockchain is the underlying technology of Bitcoin.*

> *Decentralization is achieved through Blockchain solutions.*

It is necessary to note that all the Bitcoin transactions are recorded in the distributed, replicated, and decentralized Blockchain of Bitcoin. Thus, there is not one single "Blockchain"—rather, there are many Blockchains that exist in different categories. Ethereum, for instance, has its own Blockchain. Variants of Bitcoin, which have "forked" for various reasons, have their own Blockchain.

Perhaps the best way to appreciate Blockchain decentralization (i.e., "decentralization" enabled through Blockchain), is DeFi which stands for Decentralized Finance. Much like centralized finance or banking, up to relatively recently, cryptocurrency exchanges were centralized [2]. Decentralized exchanges, such as Uniswap [3], have arrived—especially since Q3 2020. Decentralized exchanges use Automated Market Maker (AMM) [4]. Here is the core advantage [5]: "Instead of Wall Street market makers or centralized cryptocurrency exchanges collecting the lion's share of trading fees, AMMs provided returns and voting rights to anyone willing to add liquidity to a contract—whether audited or not. When before has a borrower earned a return on a debt from their lender?"

As we shall see, Decentralization has many applications besides DeFi [6]. It is one of the most critical Digital Transformation trends, especially post-COVID-19.

Blockchain Architecture

A Connected and Decentralized world involves humans, robots, and connected devices to all leverage Blockchains – especially for inter-enterprise transactions and policies. In addition to the peer-to-peer decentralized and disintermediated recording of transactions, Blockchains also execute smart contracts. Smart contracts [7] are the rules and mutual agreements between parties that get implemented in the Blockchain.

In terms of factors like the implementation, maintenance, accessibility, and consensus validation of Blockchains— there are two main categories:

- *Permissionless* or *Public Blockchains* allow anyone to join as a Blockchain node and become a consensus validator. Popular cryptocurrencies such as Bitcoin [8] and Ethereum [9] are public Blockchains.

- *Permissioned* or *Private Blockchains* require permissions for joining these Blockchain ecosystems. Typically, there are specific consortia or industry groups that leverage private Blockchains for their community.

Hyperledger Fabric [10] is one of the more popular frameworks for developing permissioned or private Blockchain solutions.

The following illustrates a robust four-layer reference architecture for innovative Permissioned or Permissionless Blockchain solutions with Smart Contracts:

- *Omni-Channel User Experience Layer*: Interaction and user experiences with Blockchain begin with the omni-channel user experience (Chapter 7) layer. Omni means "all-encompassing." This means it consistently supports different channels and all communication modes between a Blockchain service or solution provider and the customer. It also means the user can interact via a browser, mobile device, service representative, IVR (interactive voice response), or another channel consistently. This "consistency" then means that the user's experience involving the solution's capabilities is identical (unless there is a reason to provide a different channel-dependent experience).

- *Low Code/No Code Platforms Layer*: As discussed in Chapter 4, Low Code/No Code platforms have substantially evolved and altered the landscape of programming and application development—primarily through Citizen Developers' empowerment. The second layer consists of Low Code/No Code platforms for innovating and deploying Blockchain solutions. Now, even though the Low Code/No Code ecosystem involves many platforms for different objectives. At this junction, there are relatively few platforms that focus explicitly on Blockchain. It is possible to use Low Code/No Code platforms with automated integration to Blockchains. However, some Low Code/No Code platforms (Chapter 4) specifically target smart contracts. Some examples of these include Unibright [11] and Joget [12].

- *Blockchain Layer*: This is the middle layer of the three-tier architecture. It could involve one or more Blockchain implementations for specific cryptocurrency objectives. The Blockchains will execute, then, either smart contract rules or exchange cryptocurrencies for payments—*or both*. The Low Code/No Code applications will leverage Blockchain—primarily through smart contracts, with the aim being to realize a service level smart contract obligation, where financial, compliance, and time-related agreements get established between parties. The more impactful value of Blockchain is achieved through No Code applications that is a high-value mission-critical solution. The Low Code/No Code platforms layer, and the lower IoT/IIoT layer will be leveraging the Blockchain layer.

- *IoT/IIoT Connected Device Layer*: As discussed in Chapter 8, IoT/IIoT devices provide unprecedented connectivity, especially at the edges. The lowest layer will be this IoT/IIoT connectivity layer. Physical and increasingly connected devices are becoming part of robust Low Code/No Code applications. With Blockchain and IoT/IIoT edge computing, an added advantage is pushing the transactions' execution to the edges. Connected devices can potentially carry out autonomous or semi-autonomous transactions. The overall Valuechain [13] is managed and automated at the top layer, with IoT/IIoT edge computing transactions delegated to the connected devices - that can leverage Blockchain as needed.

Blockchain Intelligence

Tremendous opportunities are leveraging Artificial Intelligence (AI) for automation (Chapter 3) as well as optimizations for Low Code/No Code Blockchain applications. This is referred to and illustrated here as Blockchain Intelligence [14].

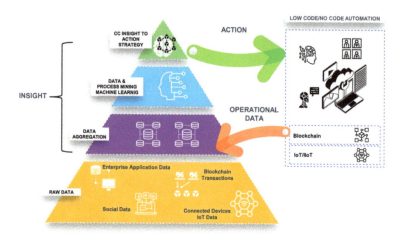

There are four primary sources of knowledge and intelligence for Blockchain:

- *Regulations, Knowledge, Policies & Procedures*: This spans the areas of operations manuals, organizational procedures, and regulatory compliance documents. Rules-based systems and language processing can be used to extract the knowledge and then operationalize it in Blockchain applications. Blockchain Smart Contracts can be leveraged to digitize the business rules involved in Policies & Procedures (e.g., by-laws or operational regulations) and execute them via Low Code/No Code applications on the Blockchain.

- *Human Intelligence*: Cognitive workers—people who use data or information to do their jobs—have a lot of deep knowledge in their heads that needs to be harvested. Blockchain Decentralized Applications [15], implemented through Low Code/No Code platforms, can utilize the Citizen Developer's [16] knowledge by digitizing business rules or through fully or semi-automated intelligent assistants.

• *Legacy Code business logic*: The embedded policies can become ossified, with little or no business visibility. They are difficult to change or extend. The challenge is to extract the intelligence in legacy systems while allowing the organization to modernize itself and be agile. Blockchain Architectures involve orchestration of smart contracts with Low Code/No Code automated API invocations of AI decisions through secure exchanges.

• Data [17]: Blockchain stores all the business transactions—including the addresses of the senders/ receivers of exchanges, if applicable, the amounts of exchanges, the meta-data of transactions, and Code execution in the Blockchain, etc. The *chain* in Blockchain only grows and is never deleted. Blocks on the chain cannot be modified. Only validated blocks can be added to the Blockchain. So, each Blockchain grows. Blockchain Data Mining [18] and Machine Learning [19] techniques with Blockchain transaction data sets are a tremendous source of intelligence.

In addition to the on-chain Blockchain data, there are several off-chain data sources: social interactions, legacy data, and IoT/IIoT data. There are specific patterns of knowledge and intelligence hidden in the aggregate of these raw data sources. The Blockchain architecture above illustrates the continuous Insight-to-Action. The "action" is realized through Low Code/No Code automation solutions. Decisions based on AI predictions can be fed back to the data source to improve the precision of the predictions in a continuous and consistent manner.

Blockchain for Inter-Enterprise Master Data Management (MDM)

Conducting business transactions across organizational boundaries has all the challenges of intra-enterprise silos and adds several others of its own. Indeed, there are often multiple versions of the "truth." Inter-Enterprise exchanges and data sharing are marred with various inefficiencies, including manual forms and paperwork, error-prone replications, delays due to organizational or bureaucratic inefficiencies, errors in language translations—especially cross-country exchanges—and difficulties and challenges in reconciling governance policies, to name a few. Hence the need for inter-enterprise Master Data Management (MDM) [20]. Blockchain is an excellent solution for inter-enterprise MDM. Here are a couple of examples:

- *Blockchain for Master KYC*: Know Your Customer (KYC) [21] is a process developed by government regulators that ensure banks and financial institutions must follow to verify the customers' identity. If a customer opens an account in, say, one bank and then wants to open another in a different financial organization, that also requires KYC—they must go through the process again. Blockchain alleviates this need by allowing even potentially competing financial institutions to share KYC information about their customers. For example, Samsung's Nexleger [22] Blockchain platform has been used by a consortium of Korean Banks to share customer identity. This provides faster, more precise, and shared KYC to all the participating banks.

- *Blockchain for Master Vehicle Identification, Registration, and History*: Another potentially huge area for inter-enterprise MDM with Blockchain is recording Vehicle Identification, processing the Registration, and the history of a vehicle on the Blockchain. These Blockchain entries can identify assets. The Blockchain can store the entire history of the vehicle's ownership, including significant events such as accidents, reports, or problems, and the driving and maintenance history. One company that is doing this is VINchain [23]. The Blockchain stores the master information and transaction about the vehicle with the given VIN. Then, all interested parties can share the master Blockchain: OEM manufacturers, distributors, dealers, owners, mechanics, DMVs, and so on.

- *Supply Chain MDM*: Supply Chain is the quintessential Extended Enterprise application domain. Interestingly, Supply Chain is also touted as an ideal use-case for Blockchain technologies [24]. Blockchain

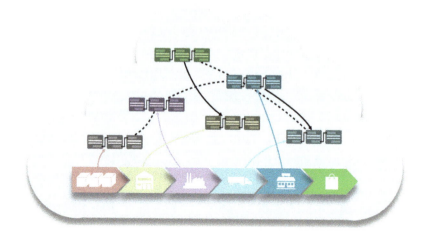

can be a good backbone [25] for Supply Chain across several essential categories of exchanges or flows: contractual flow, logistics flow (movement of goods and material), proper documentation flow, and of course—as the foundation of cryptocurrency—the financial transaction flow. The COVID-19 pandemic highlighted the vulnerabilities in supply chains when warehouses and retail stores ran out of popular items in high demand.

Blockchain and COVID-19

To review, Blockchain is a master information repository that can be shared across organizations. Organizations participating in the value chain to achieve a particular purpose, for instance, delivering goods on a supply chain—can modify or add transactions to the Blockchain.

The other essential characteristics of Blockchain include the fact that it is secure and "trustless." This term is a bit confusing, but I'll demystify it for you. It means that the parties engaged on the Blockchain have a healthy dose of mistrust toward each other—but rather than relying on a mutual trust, they can instead rely on the algorithms and the Blockchain technology to make sure the shared transactions (the "truth") on the Blockchain is reliable.

Using Blockchain effectively and focusing on the value chain—after all, Blockchain realizes the "Internet of Value"—might be one of the best technologies in directly addressing several key pandemic challenges. The Blockchain Research Institute [26] has identified several compelling use cases of Blockchain in a pandemic. These include self-sovereign identity, data sharing, just-in-time supply chain, and Rapid Response Registry for the workforce. The notion of a "self-sovereign" identity is notably impressive. The report describes it as an "inalienable digital identity, one that is neither bestowed nor revocable by any central administrator and is enforceable in any context, in-person and online, anywhere in the world." Identity through Blockchain, balancing unique identification and enforceability with privacy protection from central authorities, poses a compelling yet challenging use case.

Below, we highlight some of the more practical potential applications of post-COVID-19 Blockchain use cases.

- **Mobile, Additive, and Social Manufacturing**: These are achieved through participating in end-to-end production with 3D printing, together with social and additive manufacturing. Blockchain can be used for the exchange of components, payments, and tracking in the supply chain. It is the foundation of cryptocurrencies. There are many opportunities for trading with Blockchain. One such pragmatic example is the reconciliation and delivery of trades among several companies. Blockchain, then, can provide unprecedented accessibility and transparency of different documents (regulatory, engineering, maintenance, supply, contractual, etc.) between various participants of end-to-end Valuechains [27].

- **Food Supply Chain Traceability**: Supply chain is one of the most robust applications of Blockchain—as assets can be traced on immutable ledgers across enterprises in potentially different countries. Traceability for manufacturing parts—in conjunction with IoT and AI—can potentially address the challenges of supply chain vulnerabilities, especially under difficult circumstances such as a pandemic. More importantly, for food supply chains, traceability becomes critical and lifesaving. There are promising proposals and ideas. Meat supply chain risks could be traced through Blockchain [28]. Also, the Food Safety and Inspection Service (FSIS) commissioned IBM to develop a proof of concept with Blockchain for traceability of the food supply chain [29].

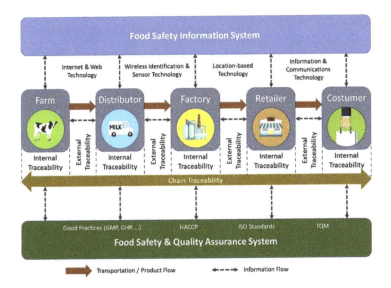

Transportation / Product Flow   Information Flow

- ***Servicing and Operations***: Provisioning the best field service technicians and continuous monitoring for optimizations can leverage Blockchain—for smart contracts, payments, and recording of operational work on the decentralized ledger. Blockchain also promotes alternative flat organizational patterns [30] for servicing and operations. Applications built on Blockchain can allow organizations to execute intelligent decisions (via smart contracts running on the Blockchain). These include proposals, recommendations, asset allocations, and votes, etc. Applications can also involve servicing employees as well as partners and even customers across multiple organizations.

- **Contact Tracing and Health Management** is a robust use case for Blockchain. The readily available and consistent identity and even potentially health records on the Blockchain, open to different respondents and health organizations, is a very compelling use case for Blockchain. For example, the UAE is an early adopter of innovative technologies, and it has adopted Blockchain for government services [31]— including healthcare, to fight COVID-19. There have also been exciting advances leveraging Blockchain in conjunction with surveillance technology elsewhere, especially in China and elsewhere For instnace, the UAE plans to have 50% of government transactions on the blockchain [32] by 2021!

- **Vaccine Supply Chain with Blockchain**: Blockchain has many synergies with IoT—the Internet of Things. The post-COVID-19 world will be both increasingly decentralized as well as optimally connected. However, even though there are success stories for applications such as Supply Chain, we still have a long way to go before we can witness the widescale global adoption of Blockchain that is possible. The next phase in the evolution for the Internet, then, is the Internet of Value, where "value" is not just monetary but also exists in the robustness of decentralized collaboration. For instance, monitoring and improving the COVID-19 Vaccine supply chain operations will be the challenge in 2021. Blockchain technology can help, but as pointed out by the World Economic Forum [33], "The difficulty does not lie in the technology, but rather in building and enlisting all of the multiple players to take part in the solution. It is in essence more of a political hurdle than a technological one."

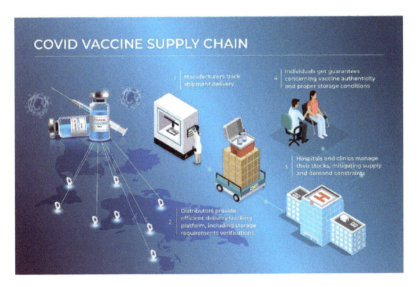

Image: Hexa Foundation [34]

Recommendations

It is true: The post-COVID-19 era is a decentralized world!

Yes, it is also connected (Chapter 8) and intelligent (Chapter 5)—but Decentralization is an essential pillar that is becoming increasingly important in the COVID-19 era.

Blockchain is therefore, the enabler of the Decentralized World. The prioritization for the Blockchain initiative depends upon the vertical sector of the organization.

However, all sectors can benefit from several common strategies.

• *Blockchain and Cryptocurrency Continuous Education*: There is still quite a bit of confusion surrounding Cryptocurrencies and Blockchain technologies in general. As illustrated in this chapter, many real-life examples could inspire you to embark upon innovative projects by leveraging Blockchain, and perhaps specific tokens or cryptocurrencies for your financial transactions or exchanges. Do your own due diligence, though. There are many organizations out there offering Blockchain or Cryptocurrency courses (primarily online) or education.

• *Blockchain Project Prioritization*: Empowered with a more robust understanding of Blockchain, you can start incorporating Blockchain solutions and technologies within your prioritized Design Thinking iterations. Blockchain—or other technologies such as IoT—will not be the core technology in most projects, but rather function as an enabler (only if it makes sense). Occasionally in your Design Thinking iterations and backlogs, you will encounter projects where Blockchain will be critical to the solution. Supply Chain is one category. The best practice Involves Design Thinking [35], Design Sprint, and Low Code/No Code MVP implementations (Chapter 6) with Blockchain components.

- *Blockchain Reference Architecture and Technology Solution mapping*: We shared the high-level, multi-tier architecture for Blockchain. It would help if you adopted this within your enterprise architecture and select tools, enablers, platforms, and capabilities for each of the layers. Examples here include Low Code/No Code platforms for Blockchain solutions, automated integration options, Blockchain, and IoT technology components. This is a tall order. The best practice involves Enterprise Architecture strategies, especially for the low-hanging fruit, prioritized projects, and your overall journey.

References

[1]   https://coinmarketcap.com/

[2]   https://www.investopedia.com/tech/what-are-centralized-cryptocurrency-exchanges/

[3]   https://uniswap.org/

[4]   https://academy.binance.com/en/articles/what-is-an-automated-market-maker-amm

[5]   https://consensys.net/insights/q3-defi-report/

[6]   https://www.coindesk.com/what-is-defi

[7]   https://www.fool.com/investing/2018/03/09/smart-contracts-and-the-blockchain-explained.aspx

[8]   https://www.bitcoin.com/

[9]   https://ethereum.org/en/

[10] https://www.hyperledger.org/use/fabric

[11] https://unibright.io/

[12] https://www.joget.org/

[13] https://cognitiveworld.com/articles/blockchain-valuechain

[14] https://www.rtinsights.com/blockchain-intelligence-ai-in-value-chains/

[15] https://www.linkedin.com/pulse/blockchain-organizational-culture-part-ii-setrag-khoshafian/

[16] https://cognitiveworld.com/articles/2020/9/27/4-no-code-citizen-developers-digital-transformation-debts-post-covid-19

[17] https://www.rtinsights.com/process-data-its-about-time/

[18] https://en.wikipedia.org/wiki/Data_mining

[19] https://en.wikipedia.org/wiki/Machine_learning

[20] https://www.rtinsights.com/blockchain-for-master-data-management/

[21]   https://en.wikipedia.org/wiki/Know_your_customer

[22]   https://www.samsungsds.com/en/blockchain-platform/nexledger.html

[23]   https://vinchain.io/

[24]   https://theiotmagazine.com/blockchain-iot-for-oil-and-gas-dx-bbcf8fb421f1

[25]   https://techcrunch.com/2016/11/24/blockchain-has-the-potential-to-revolutionize-the-supply-chain/

[26]   https://www.blockchainresearchinstitute.org/blockchain-and-pandemics/

[27]   https://www.linkedin.com/pulse/blockchain-valuechain-setrag-khoshafian/

[28]   https://cointelegraph.com/news/tracing-global-meat-related-risks-with-blockchain-amid-covid-19

[29]   https://www.sciencedirect.com/science/article/pii/S0268401219303536

[30]   https://www.rtinsights.com/blockchain-for-decentralized-autonomous-organizations-dao-covid-19-impact/

[31]   https://www.ledgerinsights.com/uae-uses-blockchain-digital-identity-to-battle-covid-19/

[32]   https://medium.com/jibrel-network/jibrel-the-uae-blockchain-strategy-2021-51d45e51b55a

[33]   https://www.weforum.org/agenda/2020/11/using-blockchain-to-monitor-covid-19-vaccine-supply-chain/

[34]   https://www.hexa.org/research

[35]   https://cognitiveworld.com/articles/2020/11/1/6-design-thinking-innovation-digital-transformation-debts-post-covid-19

Chapter 10: Competency Centers

We started with Chapter 1 with Culture. The various dimensions of the post-COVID-19 Culture included Connectivity through Virtualization, Flattening of the Organization for Empowerment, and Servant Leadership. Operational Excellence (Chapter 2) and Automation (Chapter 3) addressed the very pragmatic requirement for lean practices to alleviate Digital Transformation Debt through digital technologies. Technology is empowering everyone - "citizens" - with Low Code/No Code platforms (Chapter 4) and powerful tools for Data Science (Chapter 5).

The best defense against disruptions is Innovation through Design Thinking (Chapter 6). The Digitally Transformed organization innovates for the increasingly demanding Customers (Chapter 7).

We now reached the climax of Digital Transformation Debt—especially in the COVID-19 era: Competency Centers (aka Centers of Excellence (CoE)). Given the many complex digitization trends, a recommendation for a competency center—with a connotation of controlling and centralized—sounds somewhat contradictory, to say the least. Doesn't this run against the very core and grain of Digital Transformation?

> *"Digital Transformation requires changes to processes and thinking—changes that span your internal organizational silos. The clear delineation between technical skills and leadership skills is blurring fast." Leading Digital [1]*

In the post-COVID-19 era, alleviating Digital Transformation Debt means breaking the silos and divisions within the organization and across organizational boundaries. The blurring of technical and business skills reflects the emergence of Citizen Developers (Chapter 4) and Citizen Data Scientists (Chapter 5).

The Tug of War between Fast Innovation and Best Practices

Chapter 6 focused on Design Thinking and Innovation. As organizations try to leverage digitization, especially for customer experience optimization (Chapter 7) in an increasingly connected (Chapter 8) and decentralized (Chapter 9) world, they are often faced with a healthy tension between two compelling approaches:

- *Digital Innovation Speed*: accelerated and expressed digital application development for automation.

- *Digital Competency Best practices*: enablement, methodologies, governance, and re-use to optimize the delivery of work automation solutions.

Often, organizations pursue the next digital technology "shining object" without considering the perspective of competency—the latter is critical for success. New platforms and capabilities for Citizen Developers and Citizen Data Scientists are a strong combination of powerful and impressive innovation technologies. However, there is a certain tension between "hacking" quickly with Minimum Viable Products versus best practices for security, performance, reliability, and sustainable maintenance. As startups and enterprises attempt to accelerate their innovative initiatives in the post-COVID-19 age, it becomes even more critical to take a closer look at the core competency center enablement.

Keeping a healthy degree of tension and balance between speed and best practices is precisely the sweet spot of Digital Transformation Competency Centers. There are other dangers if an innovative startup or enterprise refuses to establish and empower a competency center— as will be discussed in the next section.

Why Competency Centers?

In a post-COVID-19 age that favors decentralization, a centralized governance body could severely limit and even suffocate innovation through unnecessary micro-management, governance, or even the bureaucracy required for approvals. However, organizations that have ignored or diminished Competency Centers have often done so at a heavy price. It could even be an existential challenge—especially when it comes to security, reliability, and governed response to customers and market trends.

Digital Transformation (DX) Competency Centers (CC) need to balance DX Strategy with pragmatic Execution Best Practices—that addresses the prioritizations and objectives of the DX Strategy.

What happens if the organizations ignore or de-emphasize the DX CC?

• Given No Code tools' proliferation, there is the danger of ad-hoc deployments with potential security, reliability, and performance vulnerabilities.

• Automation tools—particularly Robotic Process Automation—can automate non-optimized processes. The maintenance of automation, then, could become a nightmare in this context.

• Waste and inefficiencies are caused by a lack of guidance and best practice policies.

• Inconsistent performance of siloed organizations— each doing what they see best.

• Considerable waste in replicated solutions that are unnecessary: no sharing of knowledge, best practices, and re-use.

These problems could ensue when no competency center enables, governs, automates, and architects the organizational best practices across various silos or departments.

Competency Center Responsibilities and Focus

The Transformation Competency Center (DX CC) covers four key areas:

I – *Enablement and Training*: The emergence of Low Code/No Code platforms and Artificial Intelligence Machine Learning capabilities could be overwhelming. The Citizen Developers and Data Scientists need to be sufficiently trained and enabled on selected platforms for innovation, remaining responsive to customer and market trends. The DX CC is involved in choosing the best tools and platforms for Low Code/No Code and AI/ML. The DX CC trains educates and enables this new harvest of Citizen innovators – continuously.

II – *Governing Design Thinking and Design Sprint* (Chapter 6): The best practices involving continuous improvement and prioritization of Project selection, design review, and expert services:

- *Design Thinking*: This is the overarching methodology that should be platform or technology-agnostic: select, implement, and deploy the MVP that corresponds to the low-hanging fruit prioritization, and do it now!

- *Design Sprint*: This 5-day Design Sprint approach at the tail of Design Thinking Methodology aligns and realizes the Prototyping and Evaluation phases, corresponding mainly to Prototyping and Validation in a Design sprint.
- *Low Code/No Code Platform Selection*: There are now hundreds of Low Code/No Code platforms with a vast range of capabilities and pricing. The Competency Center will analyze and recommend a combination of Low Code/No Code platforms relevant to specific categories of applications.
- *Minimum Viable Product (MVP) Implementation and Deployment*: This is the ultimate objective of Design Thinking—and the beginning of the iterations for continuous improvement and market penetration. Agile methodologies are aligned to the selected platform and capabilities, with continuous iterations.

III – *Governing Automation Best Practices*: This is the governance for the adoption of automation best practices, methodologies, and guardrails to guide the DX innovation initiatives of the organization. Automation spans work that is repetitive, AI-assisted, and cognitive. As discussed in Chapter 3, COVID-19 has accentuated the need for AI-assisted work, especially as most organizations reduced customer service staffing during the pandemic and its resulting lockdowns. Organizations are increasingly relying on bots that often make the initial identification of customer issues and then involve an agent. More importantly, advanced customer service technologies are providing much-needed assistance to customer service representatives. What often occurs, is that the software robots automate the manual interactions of existing legacy systems. There should be best practice guidelines for maintaining or replacing these systems: the corresponding impact on the automation. The DX CC provides the best practices, enablement, tooling, and overall automation strategy—from mining to action in automated processes.

IV – *Optimizing the Digital Transformation Architecture*: Thus far, the 10 Chapters on Digital Transformation Debt clearly illustrate the vast potential and the complexity of digital technologies. The DX CC should also be responsible for the digital enterprise architecture. Chapter 8 and Chapter 9 presented multi-layer architecture—but that is high-level digital enterprise architecture. The comprehensive

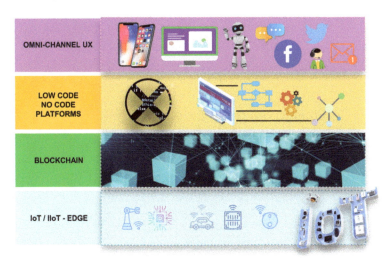

deployment architecture is much more complicated, involving components for Cloud deployments, Security, Reliability, Scalability, and DevOps modules for continuous innovation and deployment.

Here are some of the areas covered by DX Architecture best practices:

- *Legacy Modernization*: with No Code/Low Code Integration Automation platforms and modules.
- *Cloud Strategy*: On-Premises, Cloud, and Hybrid strategies and migration roadmaps.
- *Microservices*: Service-Oriented and Microservice architecture.
- *API Management:* Creating, publishing, and managing application programming interfaces.
- *Artificial Intelligence*: AI/ML modules for the DX architecture stack: different layers and components will require different AI algorithms.

  Deep learning and mining of models from data and harvesting intelligence from cognitive workers are essential components.

- *Automation*: Tools for Automation strategies and modules

The Competency Center oversees the various methodologies and iterations.

The enterprise or startup Thinks Big, Thinks Digital, and Thinks Transformation—but Starts Small: iterates and adjusts in continuous innovative iterations.

Governing, Enabling, and Accelerating Iterations

The continuous lifecycle of digital Transformation involves multiple iterations. The Digital Transformation Competency Center needs to analyze, govern, and enable the iterations for Minimum Viable Products (MVPs) and feature enhancements of existing products or services. As discussed in Chapter 6, the methodologies involve Design Thinking, Design Sprint, and Low Code/No Code MVPs.

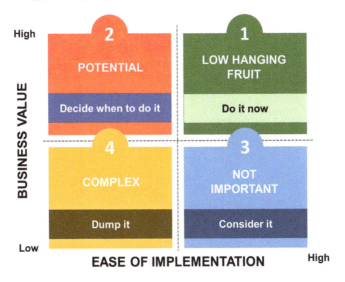

DX CC continuously monitors, iterates, and re-prioritizes various backlogs. Prioritization balances ease of implementation with business value:

- *Business Value*: How vital is the innovation project to business stakeholders? Some KPI measures include increased revenue, operational excellence for cost reduction, regulatory compliance, and customer experience optimization.
- *Ease and Complexity*: Every candidate for innovation projects will require integration with systems of record or other emerging technologies such as IoT or Blockchain. There are also other considerations such as UX complexity, scalability, security, and privacy requirements. Each of these impacts the complexities of the implementation.

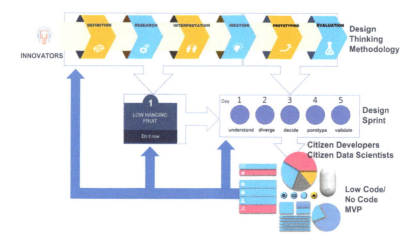

There are multiple methodologies [2]—with major and minor loops. These methodologies include prioritization through Design Thinking, Design Sprint, Agile methodology for MVP iterations, DevOps, and operational excellence Real-time Six Sigma. These are quite complex, iterative, and continuous. The importance of the DX CC to train, improve and govern the lifecycle simply cannot be overemphasized.

The methodologies, especially for delivery and productization, are iterative at their core. With a methodology such as Scrum [3], the stakeholders can provide feedback and, in some cases, might even decide to release the current version. The latter can sometimes even occur ahead of schedule—as they might deem it good enough for production. In Scrum, you will have a prioritized product backlog—a list of business and technical features that need to be implemented.

Insight to Action Iterations

As discussed in Chapter 5, the digital era is facing an unprecedented explosion of information. Digital

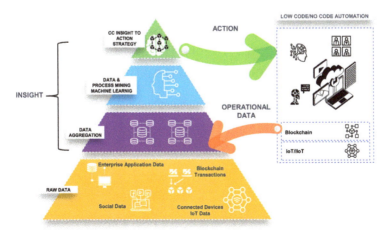

technologies, solutions, and content generate 2.5 quintillion bytes of data each day! The DX CC, then, needs to have a robust Insight-to-Action strategy. It then governs and executes the continuous raw data to aggregation to mining for insight to action continuous iterations. The Low Code/No Code automation platform realizes the "action." This continuous data-centric iteration needs to mesh with the overall innovation to MVP iterations.

Digital Transformation Competency Center Organization and Roles

An organization's DX does not happen by accident. Organizations need to understand the critical areas for accountability. Often, these are the areas that organizations assume are being accounted for as part of their DX programs and projects. However, most of the time, they are not. This further strengthens the need and business case for creating a dedicated DX CC.

Organizations by and large are convinced the "Competency Center" for aligning strategy to execution, enablement, best practices, and governance is a critical milestone in their Digital Transformation (DX) maturity roadmap.

Several organizational models and roles get involved in a DX CC. As described here [4], the organization and roles of a DX CC include:

- *DX CC Leadership*: this is the set of experienced individuals who will own, fund, and drive the direction of the DX CC.

- *DC CC Core Team*: this the group of day-to-day operations of the DX CC activities.

- *DX CC Extended Team*: this is the group of roles that, while not officially part of the DX CC, needs to be involved for the successful implementation of a DX program/project.

- *DX Project Team(s)*: Project teams will drive the day-to-day activities and understand and interact with the DC CC Core team and Extended team.

Proliferation of CCs

Organizations, by and large, are convinced that the Competency Centers for aligning strategy to execution, enablement, best practices, governance, and re-use is a critical milestone in their Digital Transformation (DX) maturity roadmap. There is a danger of Competency Center silos if every technology or methodology stakeholder unit creates a CC. It is not uncommon, therefore, to have multiple CCs for specific functional capabilities such as Big Data, Process Automation, Low Code/No Code, MDM, Cloud, AI/ML, Microservice, Mobile, Social, IoT CC, even a Blockchain CC—each attempting to achieve similar objectives but with a focus on their area. Multiple CCs with different focus areas are a painful reality.

The proliferation of CCs results in potential confusion, replication of effort, and lack of balance in the Digital Transformation Debt categories of this ten-Chapter book.

More importantly, the proliferation of CCs impedes the emergence of the autonomic enterprise in-motion [5]. These are enterprises that are both agile and anti-fragile. These are enterprises that continuously monitor measurable objectives and adjust—given various internal and external challenges. DX CC needs to enable the enterprise in motion, but without creating a suffocating governance bottleneck. A tall order indeed!

In addition to the basic organizational hierarchy illustrated above, various Competency Center models are employed to consider the organization's different functional and business units. There will also be common business applications, processes, and best practices across the various business and functional units; cross-functional teams will handle these. These models span centralized governance to more federated models with different CCs.

Recommendations

So, here we are.

We started this 10-Chapter book on alleviating Digital Transformation Debt post-COVID-19 era with Culture— the most critical dimension. We ended in this Chapter with Competency Centers. In some ways, those are the parentheses: all the other parts fit in between these two. The Culture sets the tone and direction.

The post-COVID-19 era will remain with us for many years to come. Here are the key recommendations:

- *Think Digital Transformation ... Start Small*: The most critical Digital Transformation recommendation is to take it seriously and just start the journey. However, make sure you start the journey thinking Big, thinking Digital, but *starting Small.*

- *Balance Strategy with Execution*: It is crucial to prioritize and have an overall vision and strategy. But you need to balance that with pragmatic execution. Most organizations are good at strategy. They might even create competency centers for execution. But then they either underfund or strip the DX CC of authority for execution.

- *Innovate but balance with Best Practices*: Innovation, particularly in the current climate, is the most important success requirement. Enterprises and startups should, therefore, innovate continuously to see tangible results. Do not be afraid of disrupting yourself. Be agile, be anti-fragile, and continuously measure and improve. Flatten your organization. Empower your employees and encourage them to innovate—but always balance this drive with best practices.

• *Be a data-centric Insight to Action organization*: Consider this—*Data is the new crude oil*. Most organizations do not know how to aggregate or benefit from heterogeneous data sources. Robust aggregation of data and the subsequent mining of processes or patterns are critical for success, but it should not end there. The immediate next steps are actions or executions in the context of Low Code/No Code Web and Mobile applications.

• *Do not be afraid to empower and experiment with new Organizational models—powered through Digital Technologies*: As you know by now, the post-COVID-19 era will be increasingly flattened, decentralized, and agile. Most organizations still have archaic hierarchical models. Yet even still, siloed organizations (Business, IT, Operations, Business Units, Functional Units, etc.) and siloed applications are pervasive. Empower your Citizen Developers and Citizen Data Scientists! There are unique Low Code/No Code and more robust AI platforms that can be a colossal catalyst for the organizational shift.

In conclusion, the post-COVID-19 world is becoming digitally automated, decentralized, and connected.

Enterprise Cultures need to change. Citizens need to be empowered. Innovation needs to be balanced with best practices.

The disruptions will accelerate.

We either adapt or get left behind.

It is time to alleviate the Digital Transformation Debts and start the journey!

References

[1]   https://www.amazon.com/Leading-Digital-Technology-Business-Transformation/dp/1625272472

[2]   https://www.rtinsights.com/four-intelligent-automation-methodologies-one-objective/

[3]   https://www.scrum.org/

[4]   https://www.amazon.com/Best-Practices-Knowledge-Workers-Special-ebook/dp/B01FTC8IEI

[5]   https://www.rtinsights.com/can-the-enterprise-in-motion-be-autonomic/

INDEX

A

additive manufacturing, 136

agile enterprises, 16

agility in manufacturing and supplying critical parts, 25

AI. *see* artificial intelligence (AI)

Alexa (Amazon), 34

AMM. *see* Automated Market Maker (AMM)

anti-silo transformation, 55

antifragile/anti-fragility, 81

    disposition, 53

    transformation, 55

Application Programming Interfaces (APIs), 73

    management, 152

artificial intelligence (AI), 23, 36–38, 58, 74, 111, 152

    AI-assisted work, 34–35, 150

    for automation, 129

    with digitized end-to-end value streams, 96

    models, 112, 116–117

AS. *see* automation strategy (AS)

asset monitoring and responding, 120

Atra, 58

Black Swan (Taleb), 81

Blockchain, 25, 29, 58, 83, 125, 139–140. *see also* cryptocurrency

applications, 130

architecture, 126–129, 131

and COVID-19, 134–139

decentralization, 125–126, 139

intelligence, 129–132

for inter-enterprise MDM, 132–134

layer, 128–129

permissioned, 126–127

project prioritization, 140

reference architecture, 141

Blockchain Research Institute, 135

bots, 34–35, 44, 103, 105, 150

BPM. *see* Business Process Management (BPM) and Intelligent Business Process Management (iBPM)

brainstorming techniques, 85

BTC. *see* Bitcoin (BTC)

Bubble, 57, 59

business

analysis, 71

logic, 116–117

process re-engineering, 16

stakeholders. *see* Citizen Developers

Business Process Management (BPM), 58